BRITISH COLUMBIA NATURE GUIDE

Erin McCloskey
& Gregory Kennedy

LONE PINE

Lone Pine Publishing

Lone Pine Publishing
10145 – 81 Avenue
Edmonton, AB T6E 1W9
Website: www.lonepinepublishing.com

Library and Archives Canada Cataloguing in Publication

McCloskey, Erin, 1970-
     British Columbia nature guide / Erin McCloskey

Includes bibliographical references and index.
ISBN 978-1-55105-853-5

     1. Natural history--British Columbia--Guidebooks. I. Title.

QH106.2.B7M31 2010   578.09711   C2010-900139-7

Editorial Director: Nancy Foulds
Editor: Kathy van Denderen
Technical Assistance: Krista Kagume
Production Manager: Gene Longson
Designer: Heather Markham
Layout: Janina Kuerschner
Cover Design: Gerry Dotto
Cover Images: Frank Burman, Ted Nordhagen, Gary Ross, Ian Sheldon
Illustrations Credits: see p. 4

We acknowledge the financial support of the Government of Canada through the Book Publishing Industry Development Program (BPIDP) for our publishing activities.

Disclaimer: This guide is not intended to be a "how to" reference guide for food or medicinal uses of plants. We do not recommend experimentation by readers, and we caution that a number of plants in British Columbia, including some used traditionally as medicines, are poisonous and harmful.

PC: 15

TABLE OF CONTENTS

ILLUSTRATION CREDITS

Frank Burman: 123c, 127bc, 128c, 137b, 151abcd, 153c, 155d, 156c, 157bc, 159de, 160abcd, 161abd, 164bc, 165abc, 167ab, 168abc, 169b, 170b, 172ab, 173ab, 174b, 175b, 176c, 177c, 180ab, 182ab, 184ab, 185ab, 186bc, 187abc, 188c, 189a, 190ac, 191abc, 192bc, 193c, 194c, 195bc, 196c, 197a, 198a, 200c, 201abc, 202bc, 203ab

Gary Ross: 51b, 52b, 54ab, 55a, 56ab, 57ab, 58ab, 59abc, 60abc, 61abc, 62abc, 63abc, 64ab, 65ab, 66abc, abc, 68abc, 69b, 70abc, 71abc, 72bc, 73abc, 74abc, 75ac, 76abc, 77abc, 80abc, 81abc, 82abc, 83abc, 84abc, 85ab, 86abc, 87abc, 88abc, 89ab, 90ac, 91a, 92ab, 93abc, 94b, 95abc, 96abc, 97abc, 98abc, 99a, 100bc, 101ac, 103ab, 104ab, 105abc, 106a, 107abc, 108a, 109c, 110bc, 111ab, 112ac, 113ab, 114b, 116abc, 117c, 118abc, 119abc, 120ab, 121abc

George Penetrante: 129c

Horst Krause: 72a

Ian Sheldon: 48ab, 49ab, 50ab, 51a, 52a, 53ab, 55b, 120c, 123ab, 124abc, 125abc, 126abc, 127a, 128ab, 129ab, 132abc, 133abc, 134abc, 135abc, 136abc, 137ac, 138abc, 139abc, 140abc, 141abc, 142abc, 143bc, 144abc, 145abc, 146abc, 147abc, 150abc, 152abcd, 153ab, 154abcd, 155abc, 156ab, 157a, 158abcde, 159abc, 161c, 164a, 166abc, 167c, 169ac, 170ac, 171abc, 172c, 173c, 174ac, 175ac, 176ab, 177ab, 180c, 181bc, 182c, 183abc, 184c, 185c, 186a, 188ab, 189bc, 190b, 192a, 193ab, 194ab, 195a, 196ab, 197bc, 198bc, 199abc, 200a, 202a

Ivan Droujinin: 143a

Kindrie Grove: 69ac, 75b

Linda Dunn: 181a 200b

Michel Poirier: 117a

Ted Nordhagen: 85c, 89c, 90b, 91bc, 92c, 94ac, 99bc, 100a, 101b, 102abc, 103c, 104c, 106bc, 108bc, 109ab, 110a, 111c, 112b, 113c, 114ac

ACKNOWLEDGEMENTS

Beautiful British Columbia—thanks for all those great summer family vacations! We'll move out to the coast one day, Dad!

The publisher and author would like to thank Krista Kagume for her contributions and editorial work on this title, and all the authors of earlier Lone Pine books who have created such a great library of background information.

Special thanks to Mary Borrowman of Stubbs Island Whale Watching for her comments on Pacific Coast mammals and to the following people for their assistance in the development of species lists: Dr. Louise Page, Biology Department, University of Victoria; Ian Sheldon (author and illustrator of *Seashore of British Columbia*).

MAMMALS

Orca
p. 48

Humpback Whale
p. 48

Grey Whale
p. 49

Minke Whale
p. 49

Harbour Porpoise
p. 50

Dall's Porpoise
p. 50

Pacific White-sided Dolphin
p. 51

Harbour Seal
p. 51

Northern Elephant Seal
p. 52

Northern Fur Seal
p. 52

Northern Sea Lion
p. 53

California Sea Lion
p. 53

Bison
p. 54

Mountain Goat
p. 54

Bighorn Sheep
p. 55

Dall's Sheep
p. 55

Fallow Deer
p. 56

North American Elk
p. 56

White-tailed Deer
p. 57

Mule Deer
p. 57

Moose
p. 58

Caribou
p. 58

Cougar
p. 59

Canada Lynx
p. 59

Bobcat
p. 59

Western Spotted Skunk
p. 60

Striped Skunk
p. 60

American Marten
p. 60

Fisher
p. 61

Least Weasel
p. 61

Short-tailed Weasel
p. 61

Long-tailed Weasel
p. 62

American Mink
p. 62

Wolverine
p. 62

Badger
p. 63

Northern River Otter
p. 63

Sea Otter
p. 63

Black Bear
p. 64

Grizzly Bear
p. 64

MAMMALS

Coyote
p. 65

Grey Wolf
p. 65

Red Fox
p. 66

Raccoon
p. 66

Porcupine
p. 66

Western Jumpimg Mouse
p. 67

Bushy-tailed Woodrat
p. 67

Black Rat
p. 67

Brown Rat
p. 68

House Mouse
p. 68

Deer Mouse
p. 68

Southern Red-backed Vole
p. 69

Meadow Vole
p. 69

Long-tailed Vole
p. 69

Northern Bog Lemming
p. 70

Muskrat
p. 70

Beaver
p. 70

Mountain Beaver
p. 71

Woodchuck
p. 71

Hoary Marmot
p. 71

Columbian Ground Squirrel
p. 72

Golden-mantled Ground Squirrel
p. 72

Yellow-pine Chipmunk
p. 72

Red Squirrel
p. 73

Eastern Grey Squirrel
p. 73

Northern Flying Squirrel
p. 73

Snowshoe Hare
p. 74

Mountain Cottontail
p. 74

European Rabbit
p. 74

Pika
p. 75

Masked Shrew
p. 75

Pygmy Shrew
p. 75

Virginia Opossum
p. 76

Long-eared Bat
p. 76

Little Brown Bat
p. 76

Hoary Bat
p. 77

Silver-haired Bat
p. 77

Big Brown Bat
p. 77

Snow Goose
p. 80

Canada Goose
p. 80

Tundra Swan
p. 80

Wood Duck
p. 81

Mallard
p. 81

Northern Pintail
p. 81

Green-winged Teal
p. 82

Redhead
p. 82

Lesser Scaup
p. 82

Harlequin Duck
p. 83

Surf Scoter
p. 83

Common Goldeneye
p. 83

Common Merganser
p. 84

Ring-necked Pheasant
p. 84

Ruffed Grouse
p. 84

Common Loon
p. 85

Red-necked Grebe
p. 85

Eared Grebe
p. 85

Sooty Shearwater
p. 86

Fork-tailed Storm-Petrel
p. 86

American White Pelican
p. 86

Double-crested Cormorant
p. 87

Great Blue Heron
p. 87

Turkey Vulture
p. 87

Osprey
p. 88

Bald Eagle
p. 88

Northern Harrier
p. 88

Cooper's Hawk
p. 89

Red-tailed Hawk
p. 89

American Kestrel
p. 89

Peregrine Falcon
p. 90

Sora
p. 90

American Coot
p. 90

Sandhill Crane
p. 91

Killdeer
p. 91

Black Oystercatcher
p. 91

Spotted Sandpiper
p. 92

Greater Yellowlegs
p. 92

Black Turnstone
p. 92

Western Sandpiper
p. 93

Sanderling
p. 93

Dunlin
p. 93

Long-billed Dowitcher
p. 94

Wilson's Snipe
p. 94

Wilson's Phalarope
p. 94

Bonaparte's Gull
p. 95

Ring-billed Gull
p. 95

Glaucous-winged Gull
p. 95

Common Tern
p. 96

Common Murre
p. 96

Pigeon Guillemot
p. 96

Marbled Murrelet
p. 97

11

Tufted Puffin
p. 97

Rock Pigeon
p. 97

Great Horned Owl
p. 98

Barred Owl
p. 98

Northern Saw-whet Owl
p. 98

Common Nighthawk
p. 99

Vaux's Swift
p. 99

Anna's Hummingbird
p. 99

Rufous Hummingbird
p. 100

Belted Kingfisher
p. 100

Downy Woodpecker
p. 100

Northern Flicker
p. 101

Olive-sided Flycatcher
p. 101

Pacific-slope Flycatcher
p. 101

Western Kingbird
p. 102

Northern Shrike
p. 102

Warbling Vireo
p. 102

Gray Jay
p. 103

Steller's Jay
p. 103

Black-billed Magpie
p. 103

American Crow
p. 104

Common Raven
p. 104

Horned Lark
p. 104

Violet-green Swallow
p. 105

Barn Swallow
p. 105

Black-capped Chickadee
p. 105

Chestnut-backed Chickadee
p. 106

Bushtit
p. 106

Red-breasted Nuthatch
p. 106

Winter Wren
p. 107

American Dipper
p. 107

Golden-crowned Kinglet
p. 107

Mountain Bluebird
p. 108

Swainson's Thrush
p. 108

American Robin
p. 108

European Starling
p. 109

Cedar Waxwing
p. 109

Yellow Warbler
p. 109

Yellow-rumped Warbler
p. 110

Common Yellowthroat
p. 110

Wilson's Warbler
p. 110

Western Tanager
p. 111

Spotted Towhee
p. 111

Chipping Sparrow
p. 111

Song Sparrow
p. 112

White-crowned Sparrow
p. 112

Dark-eyed Junco
p. 112

REFERENCE GUIDE

Red-winged Blackbird
p. 113

Western Meadowlark
p. 113

Brown-headed Cowbird
p. 113

Purple Finch
p. 114

House Finch
p. 114

House Sparrow
p. 114

AMPHIBIANS & REPTILES

Rough-skinned Newt
p. 116

Northwestern Salamander
p. 116

Long-toed Salamander
p. 116

Western Red-backed Salamander
p. 117

Coastal Tailed Frog
p. 117

Western Toad
p. 117

Bullfrog
p. 118

Columbia Spotted Frog
p. 118

Wood Frog
p. 118

Pacific Treefrog
p. 119

Western Painted Turtle
p. 119

Western Skink
p. 119

Northern Alligator Lizard
p. 120

Rubber Boa
p. 120

Yellow-bellied Racer
p. 120

Gophersnake
p. 121

Common Gartersnake
p. 121

Western Rattlesnake
p. 121

White Sturgeon
p. 123

Chinook Salmon
p. 123

Pink Salmon
p. 123

Kokanee • Sockeye Salmon
p. 124

Cutthroat Trout
p. 124

Rainbow Trout
p. 124

Lake Trout
p. 125

Arctic Grayling
p. 125

Mountain Whitefish
p. 125

Trout-perch
p. 126

Burbot
p. 126

Northern Pike
p. 126

FISH

Longnose Dace
p. 127

Spiny Dogfish
p. 127

Eulachon
p. 127

Black Prickleback
p. 128

Blackeye Goby
p. 128

Blue Rockfish
p. 128

Lingcod
p. 129

Tidepool Sculpin
p. 129

Pacific Sanddab
p. 129

INVERTEBRATES

Mask Limpet
p. 132

Black Tegula
p. 132

Lewis' Moon Snail
p. 132

Olympia Oyster
p. 133

Pacific Razor Clam
p. 133

California Mussel
p. 133

Lined Chiton
p. 134

Sea Lemon
p. 134

Red Sea Cucumber
p. 134

Blood Star
p. 135

Ochre Sea Star
p. 135

Eccentric Sand Dollar
p. 135

Purple Sea Urchin
p. 136

Aggregating Anemone
p. 136

Giant Green Anemone
p. 136

Orange Cup Coral
p. 137

Bread Crumb Sponge
p. 137

Moon Jellyfish
p. 137

North Pacific Giant Octopus
p. 138

Giant Acorn Barnacle
p. 138

Barred Shrimp
p. 138

Dungeness Crab
p. 139

Purple Shore Crab
p. 139

Blue-handed Hermit Crab
p. 139

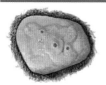
Anise Swallowtail
p. 140

Spring Azure
p. 140

Clouded Sulphur
p. 140

Pacific Fritillary
p. 141

Mourning Cloak
p. 141

Polyphemus Moth
p. 141

Common Spreadwing
p. 142

American Emerald
p. 142

Cherry-faced Meadowhawk
p. 142

Mountain Pine Beetle
p. 143

Spruce Sawyer
p. 143

Two-spot Ladybug
p. 143

INVERTEBRATES

Yellow Jacket
p. 144

Bumble Bee
p. 144

Carpenter Ant
p. 144

Giant Crane Fly
p. 145

Green Lacewing
p. 145

Cave Cricket
p. 145

Water Boatman
p. 146

Kayak Pond Skater
p. 146

Mayfly Larva
p. 146

Garden Centipede
p. 147

Cyanide Millipede
p. 147

Western Black Widow
p. 147

TREES

White Spruce
p. 150

Black Spruce
p. 150

Sitka Spruce
p. 151

Western White Pine
p. 151

Ponderosa Pine
p. 152

Lodgepole Pine
p. 152

Subalpine Fir
p. 153

Amabilis Fir
p. 153

Western Larch
p. 154

Western Hemlock
p. 154

Douglas-fir
p. 155

Western Yew
p. 155

Western Redcedar
p. 156

Yellow-cedar
p. 156

Rocky Mountain Juniper
p. 157

Arbutus
p. 157

Black Cottonwood
p. 158

Trembling Aspen
p. 158

Paper Birch
p. 159

Red Alder
p. 159

Garry Oak
p. 160

Pacific Dogwood
p. 160

Bigleaf Maple
p. 161

Douglas Maple
p. 161

Pacific Crab Apple
p. 161

Common Juniper
p. 164

Crowberry
p. 164

Scrub Birch
p. 164

Beaked Hazelnut
p. 165

Soopolallie
p. 165

Mock-orange
p. 165

Prince's Pine
p. 166

Kinnikinnick
p. 166

19

SHRUBS

Pink Mountain-heather
p. 166

Salal
p. 167

Oval-leaved Blueberry
p. 167

False Azalea
p. 167

Labrador Tea
p. 168

Bog Rosemary
p. 168

White Rhododendron
p. 168

Falsebox
p. 169

Labrador Tea
p. 168

Bog Rosemary
p. 168

White Rhododendron
p. 168

Falsebox
p. 169

Tall Oregon-Grape
p. 169

Pussy Willow
p. 169

Red-osier Dogwood
p. 170

Devil's Club
p. 170

Chokeberry
p. 170

Saskatoon
p. 171

Black Hawthorn
p. 171

Western Mountain-ash
p. 171

Trailing Blackberry
p. 172

Wild Red Raspberry
p. 172

Prickly Wild Rose
p. 172

Ninebark
p. 173

Oceanspray
p. 173

Shrubby Cinquefoil
p. 173

Birch-leaved Spirea
p. 174

Scotch Broom
p. 174

SHRUBS

Big Sagebrush
p. 174

Rabbitbrush
p. 175

Cascara
p. 175

Black Gooseberry
p. 175

Common Snowberry
p. 176

Twinflower
p. 176

Highbush-cranberry
p. 176

Black Twinberry
p. 177

Elderberry
p. 177

Western Poison-ivy
p. 177

FORBS, FERNS & GRASSES

Yellow Lady's-slipper
p. 180

Rattlesnake-plantain
p. 180

Common Blue-eyed Grass
p. 180

Wood Lily
p. 181

Nodding Onion
p. 181

Queen's Cup
p. 181

Chocolate Lily
p. 182

False Lily-of-the-valley
p. 182

Star-flowered False
Solomon's-seal
p. 182

Western Trillium
p. 183

Beargrass
p. 183

Green False-hellebore
p. 183

FORBS, FERNS & GRASSES

Meadow Death-camas
p. 184

Common Camas
p. 184

Bunchberry
p. 184

Skunk Cabbage
p. 185

Prickly-pear
p. 185

Western Spring-beauty
p. 185

Field Chickweed
p. 186

American Winter Cress
p. 186

Field Mustard
p. 186

Shepherd's Purse
p. 187

California Poppy
p. 187

Common Touch-me-not
p. 187

Northern Bedstraw
p. 188

Common Harebell
p. 188

Small-flowered
Woodland Star
p. 188

Brook Saxifrage
p. 189

Three-leaved
Foamflower
p. 189

Lance-leaved Sedum
p. 189

Common Plantain
p. 190

Cut-leaf Anemone
p. 190

Western Columbine
p. 190

Marsh Marigold
p. 191

Western Buttercup
p. 191

Western Meadowrue
p. 191

Virginia Strawberry
p. 192

Canada Violet
p. 192

Arctic Lupine
p. 192

Red Clover
p. 193

American Vetch
p. 193

Stinging Nettle
p. 193

Common Fireweed
p. 194

Common Cow-parsnip
p. 194

Northern Gentian
p. 194

Bracted Lousewort
p. 195

Spreading Phlox
p. 195

Tall Bluebells
p. 195

Scarlet Paintbrush
p. 196

Yellow Monkeyflower
p. 196

Davidson's Penstemon
p. 196

American Brooklime
p. 197

Common Yarrow
p. 197

Arrow-leaved Groundsel
p. 197

Leafy Aster
p. 198

Subalpine Fleabane
p. 198

Heart-leaved Arnica
p. 198

Canada Thistle
p. 199

Canada Goldenrod
p. 199

Coltsfoot
p. 199

FORBS, FERNS & GRASSES

Sitka Valerian
p. 200

Yellow Pond-lily
p. 200

Common Cattail
p. 200

Needle-and-thread Grass
p. 201

Water Sedge
p. 201

Common Rush
p. 201

Scouler's Surfgrass
p. 202

Common Horsetail
p. 202

Bracken Fern
p. 202

Sword Fern
p. 203

Maidenhair Fern
p. 203

Britich Columbia's natural regions are some of the most exciting and spectacular wilderness areas in the world. The province's total land and freshwater area is 95 million hectares, larger than most countries. British Columbia occupies about 10% of Canada's land surface. Foresight in establishing protected areas and provincial and national parks has conserved areas of wilderness for us to enjoy today and into the future. Beyond protected borders, parts of British Columbia are still wild enough for foxes, bears and hawks and remote enough for rare and elusive species such as bats and wolves. Our own backyards host visits from bold and opportunistic species such as coyotes, deer and many birds, insects and rodents. We are able to catch sight of whales passing close to our shores, celebrate the great spectacles of migratory birds along our Pacific Flyway in spring and autumn, wrap our arms around ancient trees in our great forests and listen to the chorus of frogs that sing within our significant wetlands, lakes and rivers. Many iconic species—the raven, bear, wolf, eagle, orca, hummingbird, frog—are totems for the Haida, the West Coast First Nations, and are representative of the cultural and natural identity of British Columbia.

British Columbia has abundant biodiversity thanks to its large and diverse landscape. It has great lengths of coastline; temperate rainforest as well as boreal forest; various mountain ranges, arid grasslands and fruit-filled Interior valleys; rivers, lakes and fresh- and saltwater wetlands; and subalpine tundra, alpine rock and ice. Even agricultural and urban areas have ecological characteristics that support or attract certain species. The unique complexities within the systems of plants and animals are governed by an infrastructure of water, soil, topography, climate and elevation, but the following eco-regions highlight the basic biogeography of the province.

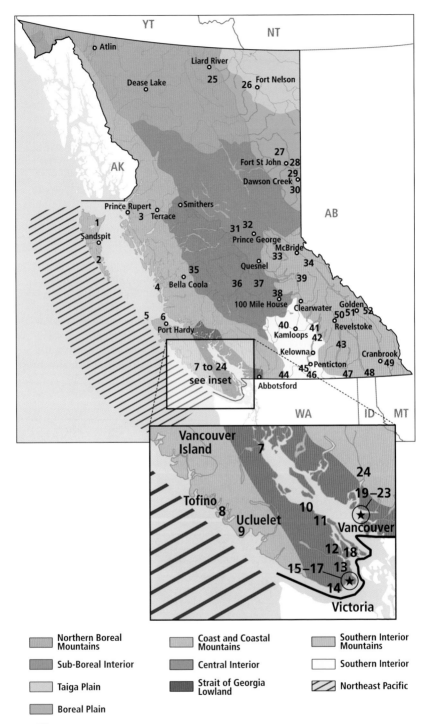

Northern Boreal Mountains

Sub-Boreal Interior

Taiga Plain

Boreal Plain

Coast and Coastal Mountains

Central Interior

Strait of Georgia Lowland

Southern Interior Mountains

Southern Interior

Northeast Pacific

Coast and Vancouver Island

1. Delkatla Wildlife Sanctuary (Masset)
2. Gwaii Haanas NP Reserve
3. Gitnadoiks River PP/Lower Skeena R.
4. Hakai Provincial Recreation Area
5. Scott Is.
6. Duke of Edinburgh Ecological Reserve
7. Courtenay/Campbell River area incl. Mitlenatch Island Nature PP and Strathcona PP
8. Tofino Mudflats
9. Pacific Rim NP Reserve
10. Parksville–Qualicum Beach WMA
11. Nanaimo, incl. Buttertubs Marsh Bird Sanctuary and Nanaimo Harbour
12. Somenos Marsh (Duncan)
13. Goldstream PP
14. Sooke area, incl. East Sooke RP and French Beach PP
15. Esquimalt Lagoon
16. Victoria, incl. Clover Pt. and Swan L.
17. Martindale Flats/Saanich Peninsula
18. Active Pass/Gulf Islands NP Reserve

Lower Mainland, Squamish

19. Burnaby L.
20. Vancouver, incl. Queen Elizabeth Park, Stanley Park/English Bay, UBC Endowment Lands
21. Iona Beach RP
22. Boundary Bay, Burns Bog, George C. Reifel Migratory Bird Sanctuary and South Arm Marshes WMA
23. Surrey, incl. Serpentine Wildlife Area and Blackie Spit
24. Brackendale Eagles PP

Northern and Central B.C.

25. Liard River area incl. Pink Mt., Stone Mt. and Muncho Lake PP
26. Ft. Nelson (along Andy Bailey Lake Rd.)
27. Beatton PP
28. Boundary L. (Peace R.)
29. McQueens Slough (Dawson Creek)
30. Swan Lake PP (Peace R.)
31. Vanderhoof Bird Sanctuary
32. Eskers PP
33. Bowron Lake PP
34. R.W. Starratt Wildlife Sanctuary and Cranberry Marsh (Valemount)
35. Tweedsmuir PP
36. Nazko Lake PP/Chilcotin Plateau
37. Scout Is. Nature Centre (Williams L.)
38. 100 Mile House Marsh Wildlife Sanctuary
39. Wells Gray PP

Southern Interior and Kootenays

40. South Thompson R./Tranquille WMA
41. Salmon Arm Bay, Shuswap L.
42. Vernon area incl. Swan Lake and Kalamalka Lake PP
43. Arrow Lakes and Hill Creek
44. E.C. Manning PP
45. Vaseux Lake Migratory Bird Sanctuary
46. Okanagan Oxbows (between Osoyoos and Oliver)
47. Pend d'Oreille Valley
48. Creston Valley
49. Kikomun Creek PP and Elko River area
50. Mt. Revelstoke NP
51. Glacier NP
52. Yoho NP

BEST SITES ABBREVIATIONS

NP = National Park	RP = Regional Park
PP = Provincial Park	WMA = Wildlife Management Area

ECO-REGIONS

Northern Boreal Mountains

The Cassiar Mountains and northern Rockies have high plateaus of alpine and subalpine tundra and deep wide valleys of muskeg and black spruce or willow-birch shrublands in cooler, less boggy areas. On the midslopes are white spruce, lodgepole pine, subalpine fir and trembling aspen. Dall's sheep can be seen on rocky alpine slopes. Grasses and forbs cover rounded summits of otherwise exposed barren rock. Some areas are in the rain shadow of the coastal mountains, but overall precipitation is balanced year-round with long cold winters and mild humid summers.

Sub-Boreal Interior

The dominant vegetation in this zone is coniferous forests of spruce, fir and pine. The sub-boreal pine-spruce zone has forests of lodgepole pine with some white spruce in the south; in the north the sub-boreal spruce zone has forests of lodgepole pine with hybrid spruce and subalpine fir common. This region is heavily forested, but it also has alpine tundra and high mountain ranges and plateaus. At low elevations, deciduous woodlands form along the rivers, streams and wetlands that are habitat for several species of fish and amphibians, and mammals such as moose and beaver. The summers are warm, but the winters are famously cold.

Taiga Plains

This eco-region crosses from the Northwest Territories into the northeastern corner of British Columbia with representation of Interior plains, some foothills and muskeg. Permafrost underlies much of the area, reducing the productivity of the soil. Slow-growing black spruce forests with Jack pine, tamarack and paper birch grow here, but shrubs such as Labrador tea, blueberry and willow are more plentiful and representative of muskeg habitat. Mammals include marten in the spruce forests and caribou and bison on the plains. Ruffed grouse are found in the riparian areas. Summers are dry but short while winters are long and cold with arctic air from the north blowing up against the foothills of the Rockies, causing snow and ice to persist for over half the year.

Boreal Plain

This eco-region is at its western extreme in northeastern British Columbia, spreading in a wide swath across part of Alberta, through central Saskatchewan and reaching its eastern extent in southeastern Manitoba, as well as extending a short distance north along the Slave River into the Northwest Territories. It is a diverse glacier-carved eco-region of northern plateaus, southern plains and rolling uplands. Plenty of lakes and wetlands provide habitat for insects, fish and migratory birds—particularly waterfowl—in the otherwise arid grasslands. Aspen and spruce make up patchy forests. The summers are warm, but the winters are cold and harsh.

Southern Interior Mountains

Snow-peaked mountains, alpine meadows and deep river valleys full of forest are the distinctive features of this eco-region in southeastern British Columbia. The Rocky Mountains to the east contain the impressive Mount Robson (at 3954 metres above sea level) and the Continental Divide (the watershed that splits the western and eastern drainage basins of North America). To the west are the Columbia Mountains, which contain several glacier-clad ranges called the Purcell, Selkirk, Monashee and Cariboo, between which are long narrow lakes such as Kootenay and Arrow and two of Canada's great winding rivers, the Fraser and the Columbia. The Columbia Mountains descend into the bountiful orchards of the Okanagan and the East Kootenay valleys. Yoho National Park in the Rockies, and Mount Revelstoke, Glacier and Kootenay national parks in the Columbia Mountains, along with the Alberta Rocky Mountain National Parks, collectively make the highest concentration of parks in any eco-region in the country—one of the largest protected natural areas in the world. Dense conifer forests of Douglas-fir, ponderosa pine, lodgepole pine, Englemann spruce and subalpine fir blanket

the lower slopes; steppe vegetation dominates major valleys and subalpine meadows; and alpine tundra is at higher elevations. Between these two mountain systems is the Rocky Mountain Trench, which funnels cold northern air through the region during winter, bringing low temperatures and high snowfall. The Columbia River wetlands in the Rocky Mountain Trench are spring and summer habitat for migratory and nesting birds and the world's highest density of breeding ospreys.

Central Interior

The Chilcotin and Cariboo plateaus, the Nechako Valley and numerous lakes create the dominant landscape of this eco-region. Mountains border south and west of this region with belts of montane containing coniferous forests of Douglas-fir, lodgepole pine forests, western hemlock and western redcedar. Extending beyond the foothills are aspen parkland and sagebrush grasslands. Several species of bats, mountain cottontail and coyote live here.

Southern Interior

The Okanagan Valley's bounty of peaches, apples and cherries occurs courtesy of the warm climate and natural irrigation by the Fraser, Skeena, Nass and Columbia rivers, which also provide excellent fish habitat. Ospreys nest in the trees and swoop over the waters with their deathly accurate fish-grabbing claws. Kootenay Lake fills the valleys of southern British Columbia's mountains, and Lake Okanagan's mythical Ogopogo, a relative of the Loch Ness monster, is sighted on rare occasion by astute (and imaginative?) observers.

Pacific Coast and Coast Mountain Range

The rocky Pacific coastline, with sandy beaches and nutrient-rich estuaries, leads from the Pacific Ocean to lush temperate forests backed by high coastal mountains with alpine tundra and glaciers. The landscape is dramatic in its beauty and its wildlife assemblage. Major cities such as Vancouver and the numerous small cities and towns along the coast strive to be borderless with the surrounding wilderness. The Coast Mountains' highest elevations, rising to well over 2440 metres—with the highest peak, Mount Waddington, at 4016 metres—have snow and icefields and glaciers up to 16 kilometres in length. The Coast Mountains pop up again as the Vancouver Island Mountains, which seldom exceed 2130 metres, but they rise abruptly from the shoreline, a stunning scene repeated along much of British Columbia's coast. The steepness of the Coast Mountains creates deep slicing fjords along the coastline, some of which extend more than 200 kilometres and rise with sheer cliffs, reaching a height of up to 2000 metres above the water. The sheltered waters of many inlets, fjords and estuaries provide habitat for marine mammals and shore life. The North Pacific Current, with upwellings of cold, nutrient-rich water from the deep ocean bottom, make animal and plant life abundant. Grey whales, migrating humpback whales, northern sea lions, harbour seals, beaked whales, orcas, sea otters, black bears, mountain lions and elk are some of the impressive array of mammals to be seen; ravens and bald eagles are iconic, and various shorebirds, including black oystercatchers, search for abundant marine invertebrates in the beaches and tidepools. The dense coastal temperate rainforests of Douglas-fir, western redcedar, western hemlock, Sitka spruce, amabilis fir and yellow-cedar contain some of the world's largest and oldest specimens. Summers are cool, with a mean annual temperature around 10°C, and winters are mild. Moisture-laden winds off the Pacific drop more precipitation here than anywhere else in Canada.

Strait of Georgia Lowland

The Strait of Georgia is a broad shallow marine basin that separates southern Vancouver Island from the mainland. The Georgia Lowlands describe a geoclimatic region that includes the Fraser Delta, Vancouver Island and smaller adjacent islands along the Strait of Georgia. This region has a mild Mediterranean climate with warm dry summers and mild winters typically lacking snow, thus permitting a great diversity of plants and animals, with several species more common in the Pacific United States at the northern extremes of their range. Migratory birds by the millions land on the mud flats and salt marshes to feed and rest before continuing their journeys while still hundreds of thousands of northern birds overwinter here. The 5.2 square kilometre Alaksen Migratory Bird Sanctuary in the Fraser Delta is a wetland of international importance—one of 30 Ramsar sites in Canada. Several charismatic mammals in this eco-region include black bear, cougar, raccoon and a small subspecies of mule deer called the black-tailed deer. Species of arbutus trees grow here, and prickly pear cacti appear on some of the Gulf Islands. The dominant forest trees are Douglas-fir, grand fir, western redcedar, lodgepole pine, Pacific dogwood (British Columbia's provincial flower), big leaf maple and red alder.

Northeast Pacific

The oceanic region off the shores of British Columbia is considered to be west of the Continental Slope to the "200 mile Economic Expansion Zone." It consists of the Continental Rise and the Continental Slope. Marine mammals in these waters include northern fur seal, Pacific white-sided dolphin and Dall's porpoise. Pelagic birds such as shearwaters spend most of their lives at sea and are rarely seen by most people. There are many oceanic fish, but species such as Pacific salmon spend part of their lives in the deep ocean and part in freshwater streams.

HUMAN-ALTERED LANDSCAPES & URBAN ENVIRONMENTS

The impact of human activity on natural environments is something we must become increasingly aware of and sensitive to as our populations continue to encroach on wildlife habitat. No brief outline of important habitats would be complete without a mention of the towns and cities of British Columbia. Roads, urban and agricultural areas and forestry and mining sites are just a few examples of our impact on the landscape. The pattern of settlement is predominantly along the coast and Vancouver Island, with smaller cities scattered throughout the islands, Rocky Mountains and the Interior.

Biodiversity is at its highest along the suburban fringe, where a botanical anarchy of remnant native plants, exotic introduced plants and hybrids exist. Strategic species, whether native or introduced, take advantage of evolving opportunities for food, shelter and breeding territory. We have established human-made lakes, urban parks bird feeders, birdhouses and bat houses to deliberately accommodate the species we appreciate, while wharves and ports, garbage dumps and our own homes seem to attract the species we don't appreciate and consider to be pests. Many of the most common plants and animals in these altered landscapes were not present before the arrival of settlers and modern transportation. The most established of the introduced species exemplify how co-habitation with humans offers a distinct set of living situations for a large number of plants and animals. House mice, Norway rats and black rats are some of the highly successful exotic animals that have been introduced to North America from Europe and Asia.

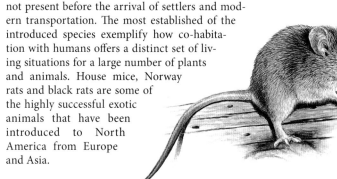

THE SEASONS

The seasons of British Columbia greatly influence the lives of plants and animals. Although some birds, insects and marine mammals are migratory, most animals are terrestrial and have varying ranges—the range of a grizzly bear can cover several hundreds of hectares while that of a vole only a few square metres. Animals with limited geographic ranges must cope in various ways with the changing seasons.

With rising temperatures, reduced snow or rain and the greening of the landscape, spring brings renewal. Many animals bear their young at this time of year. The abundance of food travels through the food chain: lush new plant growth provides ample food for herbivores, and the numerous herbivore young become easy prey for carnivores. While some small mammals, particularly rodents, mature within weeks, the offspring of large mammals depend on their parents for much longer periods.

Seeing the spring flowers colouring the landscape is a seasonal treat when the province is in full bloom. Locations such as the grasslands and fruit orchards of the Okanagan Valley or the subalpine meadows of the Rockies attract hikers and photographers. Pollinators such as bees and butterflies are naturally also to be seen, as well as the many mammals attracted to the fresh young forbs, grasses and flowers to graze upon (note that bears are particularly active at this time of year in subalpine wildflower meadows). There are also many excellent botanical gardens in British Columbia to see native plants in full spring flower.

During summer, animals have recovered from the strain of the previous winter's food scarcity and spring's reproductive efforts, but it is not a time of relaxation. To prepare yet again for the upcoming autumn and winter, some animals must eat vast quantities of food to build up fat reserves, while others work furiously to stockpile food caches in safe places. Some of the more charismatic species, such as elk—the bugling bull demonstrates extremes of aggression and vigilance—mate in autumn, and some small mammals, such as voles and mice, mate every few months or even year-round.

Winter differs in intensity and duration throughout these two states. In coastal and southern areas, winters are mild and do not create much stress for animals. The Interior region with increasing snow and decreasing temperatures farther north and in higher mountain elevations can make winter an arduous, life-threatening challenge for many creatures. For herbivores, high-energy foods are difficult to find, often requiring more energy to locate than they provide in return. This negative energy balance gradually weakens most herbivores through winter, and they in turn provide food for the equally needy carnivores. Voles and mice also find advantages in the season—an insulating layer of snow protects their elaborate trails from the worst of winter's cold. Food, shelter and warmth are all found in the thin layer between the snow and the ground surface, and the months devoted to food storage now pay off.

The seasons also affect species composition. The array of species differs from west to east and from winter to summer in those regions. When you visit the Interior or mountainous regions in winter, for example, you will see a different group of species than in summer: plants die back, migrating animals head south, and other animals become dormant in winter; conversely, many species of birds arrive at winter bird feeders, and certain mammals, such as deer, enter lowland meadows to find edible vegetation, making these species more visible in winter.

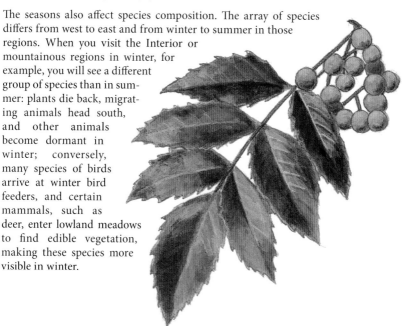

OBSERVING NATURE

Many animals are most active at night, so the best times for viewing them are during the "wildlife hours" at dawn and at dusk when they emerge from their daytime hideouts or roosting sites. During winter, hunger may force some mammals to be more active during midday. Conversely, in warm seasons, some animals may become less active and less visible in the heat of the day. Within the protected reserves and national parks of British Columbia, some of the larger mammals can be viewed easily from the safety of a vehicle. If you walk backcountry trails, however, you are typically in the territory of certain mammals with which encounters are best avoided unless from a distance.

Birdwatching is a popular activity among serious "birders" and people who simply wish to recognize and appreciate the diversity of attractive and interesting birds. Guidebooks, online resources and clubs and organizations are all abundant and accessible for those interested in learning more about local birdlife. Birdwatching is both relaxing and a ready source of mental and physical exercise. British Columbia's geographical diversity hosts many breeding and year-round residents and large numbers of spring and autumn migrants. To date, 502 bird species have been recorded in British Columbia; 312 of these bird species breed in the province, which is almost three-quarters of all the bird species breeding in Canada. Several ecological reserves grant protected nesting habitat for British Columbia's five million nesting seabirds. In addition, about one-quarter of these breeding birds are habitat generalists and can be seen throughout much of the province. Even in winter, British Columbia's mild climate permits numerous bird species to overwinter along the south coast and allows the Christmas bird count to tally up to 180 species, to the envy of the rest of Canada. One must be patient, though, because birds are highly mobile animals; they may be seen one moment and then vanish the next!

Whale watching can be an organized activity, with boats taking groups of tourists out to known areas of high whale and dolphin sightings, or, because many species frequent inshore waters, it can be a random moment of fortune right from the

shore. Although whale watching has strong merit for encouraging public aware-ness and appreciation for marine mammals and the health of the oceans, it can disrupt cetacean behaviour, and tour groups must be considerate and passive in the presence of these sensitive species.

Although more people have become conscious of the need to protect wildlife, human pressures have nevertheless damaged critical habitats, and some species experience frequent harassment. Modern wildlife viewing demands courtesy and common sense. Honour both the encounter and the animal by demonstrating a respect appropriate to the occasion. Here are some points to remember for ethical wildlife watching in the field:

- Stress is harmful to wildlife, so never chase or flush animals from cover or try to catch or touch them. Use binoculars and keep a respectful distance, for the animal's sake and often for your own. Amphibians are especially sensitive to being touched or held—sunscreen or insect repellent on your skin can poison the animal.

- Leave the environment, including both flora and fauna, unchanged by your visits. Tread lightly and take home only pictures and memories. Do not pick wildflowers, and do not collect sea stars, sea urchins or seashells still occupied by the sea animal.

- Fishing is a great way to get in touch with nature, and a lot of anglers appreciate the non-consumptive ethos of catch-and-release.

- Pets hinder wildlife viewing. They may chase, injure or kill other animals, so control your pets or leave them at home.

- Take the time to learn about wildlife and the behaviour and sensitivity of each species.

- Consider that even city parks offer ample opportunity to revel in nature and see many species of plants and animals.

NATIONAL PARKS & PROTECTED AREAS

A significant 14.26% (or more than 13.5 million hectares) of British Columbia's land base is protected—more than any other province in Canada. Millions of visitors per year spend time in British Columbia's parks; hiking, biking, canoeing, kayaking and camping are a few of the ways to explore the parks and submerse oneself in nature. Each park, from those on the coast to those in the mountains, has its own special beauty and ecological importance.

1. **Gwaii Haanas National Park Reserve** is on the Queen Charlotte Islands (Haida Gwaii) of northern British Columbia. These islands are the ancestral home of the Haida—the West Coast First Nations—who have lived here for thousands of years. The islands have a diverse natural and cultural history, where totems and old-growth forests survive. The park was established in 1988 after local people, fellow Canadians and the international community rallied support for the Haida to have the islands protected from devastating logging practices. Skung Gwaii in the southern half of the park is a UNESCO World Heritage Site with the world's largest collection of totem poles still standing in their original location. Old-growth dependent species also survive, including downy and resident subspecies of hairy woodpeckers. Gwaii Haanas protects the habitat of 39 species of endemic plants and animals. Bald eagles, black bears, orcas and other totemic animals are appropriately abundant here.

2. **Pacific Rim National Park** is on the west side of Vancouver Island and includes Tofino, Ucluelet and Bamfield. When this park was established in 1970, there were few inhabitants and very little infrastructure such as roads throughout its 49,962 hectares of nationally protected area. Today, over one million visitors per year travel on the Pacific Rim Highway to experience this remote and breathtaking landscape of old-growth coastal temperate rainforest (with precipitation among the heaviest in the world) along the long rugged coastline onto the expansive and dynamic Pacific Ocean. The Native inhabitants are the Nuu-chah-nulth peoples. Bird- and whale-watching are prime activities here to observe migratory birds and several species of whale, and you can spend hours exploring the tide pools.

3. **Gulf Islands National Park** was granted national park status in 2003 to protect portions of 15 of British Columbia's southern Gulf Islands, including Saturna, Mayne and Pender, many islets and reefs as well as 26 km^2 of marine areas. Brackman Island has remained unaltered from livestock grazing, logging or settlement and has old-growth stands of forest with individual trees up to 250 years old. The Channel Islands are important seal and sea lion haul-outs and bird nesting areas. Hiking, kayaking, cycling and camping are popular ways to explore this area and take in its natural beauties and diversity.

4. **Mount Revelstoke, Glacier** and **Yoho** national parks are adjacent to one another in the eastern reaches of the southern Interior's Rocky Mountains. Mount Revelstoke National Park contains the Monashee and Selkirk ranges with high alpine plateaus and subalpine meadows full of wildflowers in summer. There is only backcountry camping in this park but plenty of day-use opportunities to hike, cross-country ski or picnic (be bear-safe). Old-growth forests have 800-year-old cedar trees, and wetlands provide migratory bird habitat. May and June are the best months for birdwatching: Steller's jay, chestnut-backed chickadee, western tanager, American dipper, rufous hummingbird, yellow warbler, common yellowthroat and Pacific-slope flycatchers in the wetlands; black-capped and chestnut-backed chickadees, Swainson's thrush, olive-sided flycatcher and gray jay in the subalpine meadows; and various species of thrush and the western tanager at the foot of Mount Revelstoke. Hike through the valleys below the Illecillewaet and Asulkan

glaciers in Glacier National Park where more than 400 glaciers carve out the Columbia Mountains and fill the glacier-fed rivers. Glacier National Park is known as the birthplace of mountaineering in North America, since British mountaineers Green and Swanzy first climbed the Selkirks. Go ice-waterfall climbing in winter or searching for fossils in summer in Yoho National Park, on the British Columbia/Alberta border. Yoho is characterized by waterfalls, glacial lakes, snow-capped mountains riddled with caves and tunnels, deep forests, natural rock bridges spanning roaring rivers and hoodoos.

In addition to national parks, British Columbia has nearly 1000 provincial parks and protected areas encompassing more than 1.9 million hectares. Each of these parks and significant habitats aim to conserve the diversity of unique flora, fauna and geography found throughout the province. While national parks grant protection from industry, development and hunting activities, and control commercial and residential growth, there are three classes of provincial parks: fully protected natural or historic parks in which no commercially extractive industrial uses are permitted; parks where discreet and regulated resource extraction is allowed; and small parks that are mainly for local, primarily recreational use near urban areas and afford habitat for small animals and young vegetation but are not large enough to hold ecosystem value. Hunting and fishing is permitted with a licence in many provincial parks; activities such as mushroom picking or harvesting is prohibited. The following list is a sampling of parks, beyond those shown on the map on p. 28, which are noteworthy for having rare habitats, local abundance of specific species or record-setting special features.

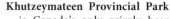

Khutzeymateen Provincial Park is Canada's only grizzly bear sanctuary. It protects a population of approximately 50 bears in this one area, which is the highest known concentration of grizzly bears along the British Columbia coast.

Liard River Hot Springs Provincial Park includes the hot springs ranked second largest in Canada and in the top five in North America. The pools' water temperatures range from 42° to 52°C. The park protects boreal spruce forest; however, a rare warm-water swamp around the springs creates a unique plant and insect biodiversity and attracts mammals such as moose. These swamps do not freeze in winter despite being at a latitude of nearly 60° N.

Manning Provincial Park is a popular recreational destination in British Columbia with easy access to an abundance of nature-based activities and wildlife viewing opportunities. It is located in a transition zone between wet coastal ranges and the dry Interior plateau, so a diversity of habitats and species (such as deer, bears, wolverines and beavers) are found here.

Mount Assiniboine Provincial Park has been referred to as Canada's Matterhorn. This backcountry park is for intrepid outdoors people who can access the park by foot or horseback. The reward is a true nature experience complete with the calls of howling wolves.

Mount Robson is the highest peak in the Canadian Rockies at 3954 metres; the provincial park named in its honour also contains the Berg Glacier. Trails in this park connect with those in Jasper National Park, AB.

Roderick Haig-Brown Provincial Park is where the sockeye salmon run can be viewed.

Spatsizi Plateau Wilderness Provincial Park includes one of British Columbia's most important habitats for woodland caribou.

Stone Mountain Provincial Park is the highest elevation pass of the Alaska Highway.

Strathcona Provincial Park was British Columbia's first provincial park, established in 1911. Within this park, the largest on Vancouver Island, are Della Falls; tumbling and crashing over a drop of 440 metres, this waterfall is arguably the highest in Canada and is among the highest in the world.

Tatshenshini-Alsek Provincial Park is a World Heritage Site; its 947,026 hectares combined with adjacent parks in Alaska and the Yukon form the world's largest international World Heritage Site.

Tweedsmuir Provincial Park is British Columbia's largest provincial park at 989,616 hectares. It was established in 1939 and is located in the Coast Range. Black bears, cougars and old-growth cedars are among the diversity of flora and fauna. While Tweedsmuir is impressively the largest provincial park, the smallest in British Columbia, at less than one hectare, is **Memory Island**.

Vaseux Lake Provincial Park and **Vaseux-Bighorn National Wildlife Area** give recognition to the rare dry grassland ecosystems of native grasses and other plants, which are considered the most threatened by invasive species in western Canada. Endangered tiger salamanders and threatened pallid bats are members of this ecosystem. More commonly observed are bighorn sheep and rattlesnakes.

Wells Gray Provincial Park is often referred to as the Waterfall Park for its countless cascades, rapids, torrents and waterfalls. Most noteworthy is Helmcken Falls, which is three times the height of Niagara Falls. Also in this 540,000-hectare park is Murtle Lake, the largest lake in North America to only permit canoes and no motorized watercraft.

In addition, the **Muskwa-Kechika** is a one-million hectare wilderness management area that is part of the Yellowstone to Yukon initiative to connect vital migratory corridors throughout the Rockies. These critical habitat zones of boreal plain, muskeg, alpine and montane connect and allow far-roaming species such as the grizzly bear and wolf access to prey populations and to establish individual territories for mating and raising young, while management tries to mitigate the dangers of perilous road and rail crossings or human conflicts.

Kitlope Heritage Conservancy protects central coastal British Columbia's Kitlope Valley (321,120 hectares), part of the largest intact coastal temperate rainforest in the world. Coastal temperate rainforest is an extremely rare ecosystem globally, with 60% of the original area destroyed by logging and development, and contains twice the amount of biomass per square metre as tropical rainforests. Seven million hectares of coastal temperate rainforest on the northwest coast of British Columbia remain unprotected. Near 100-metre-high trees, well over 1000 years old, are sentinels of this old-growth forest ecosystem, which provides unique habitat for wild salmon, eagles, grizzly bears, wolves and the beautiful "Spirit Bear," a rare white subspecies of the black bear and British Columbia's official mammal.

Sometimes wildlife areas are ecologically significant protected areas for scientific and educational/research purposes with very limited human recreational opportunity. Ecological reserves are one

such example, and there are dozens within British Columbia. Anne Vallee (Triangle Island) Ecological Reserve protects 1980 hectares of habitat at the northern tip of Vancouver Island and contains the largest seabird colony in British Columbia and the largest orthern sea lion colony in Canada (second largest in the world). The nesting birds are so sensitive to human disturbance that this ecological reserve is closed to the public.

Other significant wilderness areas, despite international recognition and local appeal, remain unprotected. One such place worthy of mention is Clayoquat Sound on the west coast of Vancouver Island. Herein contains 3500 km^2 (land and water area) of intact/unlogged temperate rainforest, the largest left on Vancouver Island. This coastal old-growth forest provides habitat for wolves, black bears, cougars, orcas, bald eagles, ospreys, marbled murrelets and other endangered species. Although the Pacific Rim National Park Reserve and parts of Strathcona Provincial Park are within the Sound, outside of these parks there is no legal habitat protection. Decisions by the British Columbia government in 1993 to allow clear-cut logging resulted in the largest act of peaceful civil disobedience in Canadian history when thousands of protesters blocked logging roads and brought world recognition to the Sound. The Sound was deemed a UNESCO Biosphere Reserve in 2000; logging, however, continues today.

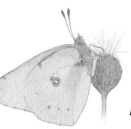

ANIMALS

Animals are mammals, birds, reptiles, amphibians, fish and invertebrates, all of which belong to the Kingdom Animalia. They obtain energy by ingesting food that they hunt or gather. Mammals and birds are endothermic, meaning that body temperature is internally regulated and will stay nearly constant despite the surrounding environmental temperature unless that temperature is extreme and persistent. Reptiles, amphibians, fish and invertebrates are ectothermic, meaning that they do not have the ability to generate their own internal body temperature and tend to be the same temperature as their surroundings. Animals reproduce sexually, and they have a limited growth that is reached at sexual maturity. They also have diverse and complicated behaviours displayed in courtship, defence, parenting, playing, fighting, eating, hunting, in their social hierarchy, and in how they deal with environmental stresses such as weather, change of season or availability of food and water. We have included the region's most common, wide-ranging, charismatic or historically significant animals and have chosen a few representatives for diverse families such as rodents.

MAMMALS

Mammals are the group to which human beings belong. The general characteristics of a mammal include being endothermic, bearing live young (with the exception of the platypus), nursing their young and having hair or fur on their bodies. In general, all mammals larger than rodents are sexually dimorphic, meaning that the male and the female are different in appearance by size or other diagnostics such as antlers. Males are usually larger than females. Mammals are grouped as herbivores, carnivores, omnivores or insectivores. People often associate large mammals with wilderness, making these animals prominent symbols in Native legends and stirring emotional connections with people in modern times.

Marine Mammals
pp. 48–53

Bison
p. 54

Hoofed Mammals
pp. 54–58

Cats
p. 59

Skunks & Weasels
pp. 60–63

Bears
p. 64

Dogs
pp. 65–66

Raccoon
p. 66

Porcupine
p. 66

Mice, Rats & Kin
pp. 67–70

Beaver & Muskrat
p. 70

Mountain Beaver
p. 71

Squirrels
pp. 72–73

Hares & Pikas
pp. 74–75

Shrews
p. 75

Opossum
p. 76

Bats
pp. 76–77

Orca

Orcinus orca

Length: 8–10 m
Weight: 7.2 tonnes

The iconic orca is the largest member of the dolphin or toothed whale family and one of the most well-known whales worldwide. Researchers have identified 3 distinct types of orcas along the Pacific coast: transients, residents and less-researched offshore types. Differences include diet, home range and social behaviour. Resident orcas occur mainly in sheltered, coastal waters, prefer to feed on fish and tend to be very vocal. Transient orcas travel farther, from Alaska to Monterey Bay, CA. Stealthy transients hunt silently, feeding mainly on marine mammals such as seals and sea lions, and vocalize after they have made a kill. **Where found:** cool coastal waters, inshore and offshore. **Also known as:** killer whale.

Humpback Whale

Megaptera novaeangliae

Length: 14–18 m
Weight: 31–41 tonnes

The haunting songs of humpbacks can last from a few minutes to a few hours or even be epic, days-long concerts; they have inspired both scientists and artists and reach out to the imaginations of many people who listen and wonder what these great creatures are saying. • These whales employ a unique hunting strategy: they make a bubble net to round up their prey, then swim open-mouthed through the clustered food supply. **Where found:** off our shores in summer; migrate in winter to the waters off Mexico or Costa Rica, some to Hawaii, to mate and calve.

Grey Whale

Eschrichtius robustus

Length: 10–15 m
Weight: 18–36 tonnes

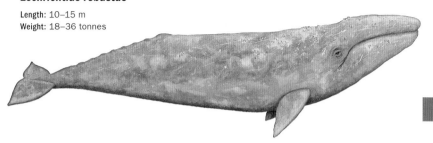

Grey whales are famous for their lengthy migrations that take them between the Arctic seas in summer and the Mexican coast in winter, thrilling whale watchers along the entire Pacific Coast as they pass by. Resilient grey whales have bounced back twice from near extinction, once in the 1860s and again in the 1920s. West coast populations have recovered, but the Asian population remains critically endangered. • This baleen whale has grey skin covered with a speckling of barnacles and carries large communities of other organisms, such as whale lice, along for the ride. **Where found:** generally coastal waters, as it migrates close to shore.

Minke Whale

Balaenoptera acutorostrata

Length: 8–9 m
Weight: 5–7 tonnes

Smallest of the rorquals—baleen whales with throats of pleated, expandable skin—the minke whale is occasionally seen in our waters, but it spends little time at the water's surface, so a fleeting glimpse is a lucky one. • The minke whale has been one of the more heavily hunted of the baleen whales since the 1980s, when larger whale populations had already collapsed. **Where found:** open water, sometimes in bays, inlets and estuaries; migrates seasonally between warm and cold waters.

Harbour Porpoise

Phocoena phocoena

Length: average 1.4 m
Weight: average 40 kg

Once a familiar sight, the harbour porpoise has been declining worldwide. Although harbour porpoises are caught in offshore nets and suffer from inshore pollution, reasons for their decline are not well known. • This small porpoise usually occurs singly or in small groups and feeds mainly on squid and fish, with groups sometimes working cooperatively to herd schooling fish. Larger groups of up to 60 porpoises may gather in summer and early autumn. **Where found:** sheltered, inshore waters, occasionally travels up large rivers.

Dall's Porpoise

Phocoenoides dalli

Length: males 1.8–2.4 m
Weight: average 125 kg

The striking black-and-white pattern of the Dall's porpoise has earned it the nickname "baby orca," but the Dall's porpoise has a different colour pattern, including a white-tipped dorsal fin and white trailing edge on the flukes. • This steady swimmer, capable of reaching 30 knots (55 km/h), is not shy of humans and will sometimes swim alongside boats. When surfacing to breathe, the Dall's porpoise creates a unique spray pattern known as a rooster tail. **Where found:** offshore and partially sheltered, inshore waters.

Pacific White-sided Dolphin

Lagenorhynchus obliquidens

Length: 2.1–2.4 m
Weight: 90–140 kg

Whale watchers lucky enough to see Pacific white-sided dolphins often get some bonus entertainment from these highly acrobatic animals: breaching, somersaulting and bow-riding, seemingly very excited at the opportunity to show off. • Dolphins can focus their vision above and below water and often take a closer look at people by jumping alongside the boat or lifting their heads above the water's surface. **Where found:** coastal and larger sheltered waters, especially on the inside straits between islands and the mainland.

Harbour Seal

Phoca vitulina

Length: 1.7 m
Weight: 100 kg

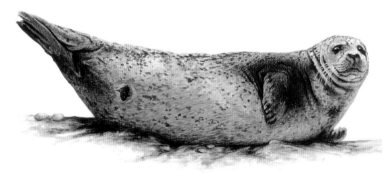

Year-round, great colonies of harbour seals can be observed either basking by day or sleeping at night on rocky shores and islands. Oftentimes during the day, individuals can be seen bobbing vertically in the water—the harbour seal cannot sleep at the surface in the manner in which sea otters can, but they can actually sleep underwater, going without breathing for up to 30 minutes. • Harbour seals are shy of humans but do occasionally pop their heads up beside a canoe or kayak to investigate, usually making a quick retreat thereafter. **Where found:** bays and estuaries, intertidal sandbars and rocky shorelines along the coast.

Northern Elephant Seal

Mirounga angustirostris

Length: *Male:* 3.7–4.9 m; *Female:* 2.1–3.7 m
Weight: *Male:* up to 2300 kg; *Female:* up to 900 kg

The northern elephant seal is the show-off of the seal family. The largest seal on our coast, it dives to depths of more than 1500 m in search of food and is able to hold its breath for up to 80 minutes. A far-ranging male may cover 21,000 km, spending more than 250 days at sea, in migrating between its northern feeding waters and its winter breeding and moulting beaches in California and Mexico.
• Both sexes sport a large snout, but that of the adult male is a pendulous, foot-long "trunk" that produces impressive rattling snorts. **Where found:** offshore, resting at the surface of the water.

Northern Fur Seal

Callorhinus ursinus

Length: *Male:* 1.8–2.3 m; *Female:* 1.1–1.5 m
Weight: *Male:* 150–280 kg; *Female:* 38–54 kg

Completely at home in the ocean, the northern fur seal almost never comes to shore, except to breed on rocky islands in the Bering Sea. For the remaining 7–10 months of the year, this pelagic seal typically travels the sea alone, covering up to 10,000 km a year. This wide-ranging species is found from California up the Pacific coast and across the North Pacific to Japan. To see these seals, a boat trip is required off the west coast of Vancouver Is., the Queen Charlottes or Hecate Strait during migration. **Where found:** offshore waters.

Northern Sea Lion

Eumetopias jubatus

Length: *Male:* 2.6–3.4 m; *Female:* 1.8–2.1 m
Weight: *Male:* up to 1000 kg; *Female:* 270–360 kg

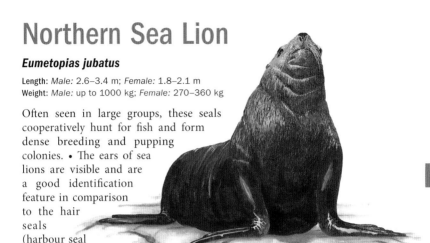

Often seen in large groups, these seals cooperatively hunt for fish and form dense breeding and pupping colonies. • The ears of sea lions are visible and are a good identification feature in comparison to the hair seals (harbour seal and elephant seal), whose ears are not visible externally. • Northern sea lions may be seen around Bellhouse PP, Nanaimo Harbour, Mayne Is., Pender Is., French Beach PP, Pacific Rim NP and Gwaii Haanas NP Reserve. **Where found:** coastal waters near rocky shores; may rest in the water in a vertical position. **Also known as:** Steller sea lion.

California Sea Lion

Zalophus californianus

Length: *Male:* 2–2.5 m; *Female:* 1.5–2 m
Weight: *Male:* 200–390 kg; *Female:* 45–110 kg

California sea lions are the playful sea mammals that regularly perform at marine aquariums, leaping through hoops or balancing balls on the nose. These pinnipeds are naturally playful, and wild females and pups frequently play and body surf in the waves. California sea lions reach the northern extension of their range in B.C., so they are generally rare. But from October to February at certain haul-out sites on the southeastern side of Vancouver Is., wintering males can be common. **Where found:** coastal waters with rocky or sandy beaches of south B.C. coast.

Bison

Bison bison

Length: 2.4–3.9 m
Shoulder height: 1.6–1.8 m
Weight: *Male:* 640–910 kg; *Female:* 490–570 kg

North America's largest native land mammal, the bison literally weighs a tonne. Before the arrival of the Europeans, great herds totalling millions of bison roamed parts of western North America. By the early 1900s, overhunting, disease, severe winters and interbreeding had devastated their numbers and extirpated these noble beasts from much of their range. Today, the vast majority of bison are raised in private herds, restricted to ranches or protected areas. • Two subspecies exist: the wood bison *(B. b. athabascae)* and the plains bison *(B. b. bison).* **Where found:** free-ranging herds in northeastern B.C. include those along the north and west lowlands of Pink Mountain; between Beatton and Halfway rivers; and Liard River.

Mountain Goat

Oreamnos americanus

Length: 1.2–1.5 m
Shoulder height: 90–120 cm
Weight: 45–135 kg

Watching a mountain goat climb or descend the steep rocky slopes of their high alpine home can leave observers feeling on edge, but this animal is more than comfortable on precarious cliffs and high precipices. A mountain goat's anatomy is such that it can place and maneuvre all 4 hooves on a ledge as small as 15 x 5 cm. • Within hours of birth, playful mountain goat kids are able to run, jump and climb. **Where found:** steep slopes and rocky cliffs in alpine or subalpine areas throughout the Coastal and Rocky mountains.

Bighorn Sheep

Ovis canadensis

Length: 1.5–1.8 m
Shoulder height: 75–115 cm
Weight: 55–155 kg

Male bighorn sheep have spectacular horns that they use in head-butting clashes during fall rut. Both sexes have brown horns, but the females' are short and do not curve around as impressively as the males'. • Mountain meadows provide feeding grounds, and rocky outcroppings provide protection from predators—eagles, mountain lions and bobcats—which prey on the lambs. **Where found:** rugged mountain slopes, cliffs and alpine meadows; Rocky Mountains of east-central B.C.

Dall's Sheep

Ovis dalli

Length: 1.4–1.8 m
Shoulder height: 75–105 cm
Weight: 45–100 kg

Two distinct races of Dall's Sheep occur in B.C.: the darker, more common Stone Sheep (ssp. *stonei*) of northern B.C. and the white *dalli* ssp. of extreme northwestern B.C. Identified by their long, wide-spreading spiral horns, Dall's sheep are found in the mountains and highlands of northern British Columbia. They are sometimes called "thinhorn sheep," because the rams' horns are relatively thin at the base compared with the massive horns of bighorn sheep. When rams engage in their fall head-butting contests, the sound of their horns clashing can be heard more than 2 km away. Dall's ewes have much smaller horns. **Where found:** northern B.C.; alpine tundra, mountains, highlands.

Fallow Deer

Dama dama

Length: 1.4–1.8 m
Shoulder height: about 1 m
Weight: 40–80 kg

With populations in at least 38 countries, the fallow deer of Europe and Central Asia is one of the most widely introduced ungulates in the world. In B.C. it occurs on several of the Gulf Is., where it has no predators. This adaptable deer was originally introduced to North America for hunting purposes or as an attractive addition to public parks, but introductions have resulted in a decline of native deer in some areas. • Fallow deer are farmed throughout the province, especially in the Thompson-Okanagan region. **Where found:** some Gulf Is., including Sidney Is. and James Is.; various habitats.

North American Elk

Cervus elaphus

Length: 1.8–2.7 m
Shoulder height: 1.7–2.1 m
Weight: 180–500 kg

The impressive bugle of the male North American elk once resounded throughout much of the continent, but the advance of civilization pushed these animals west. Today, elk are common in the Rocky Mountains and are scattered locally elsewhere. • During the autumn mating season, rival males use their majestic antlers to win and protect a harem of females. An especially vigorous bull might command more than 50 females. After the rut, bull elk can put on as much as 1 kg every 2–3 days if conditions are good. The extra weight helps them survive winter. **Where found:** grasslands or open woodlands; eastern B.C.; scattered along the Pacific Coast, including Vancouver Is. **Also known as:** wapiti.

White-tailed Deer

Odocoileus virginianus

Length: 1.4–2.1 m
Shoulder height: 70 cm–1.1 m
Weight: 30–115 kg

White-tailed deer populations have boomed in many areas of Canada. Easily our most abundant hoofed mammal, they are even found in urban and suburban areas, often near forested tracts, wooded ravines or river valleys. When startled, white-tails bound away flashing their conspicuous white tail. • Feeding does (females) leave their speckled, scentless fawns in dense vegetation to hide them from predators. • Bucks (males) regrow their racks, or antlers, each year and can develop massive racks with age.
Where found: most habitats except the densest forests; eastern B.C.

Mule Deer

Odocoileus hemionus

Length: 1.4–1.7 m
Shoulder height: 90–105 cm
Weight: *Male:* 50–215 kg; *Female:* 30–75 kg

Gentle and often approachable, mule deer frequent open areas or parks, where they are wonderful to watch. They travel with a characteristic, bouncing gait, launching off and landing on all fours at the same time. • As their name suggests, mule deer have very large ears. Their white rump patch and black-tipped tail distinguish them from white-tailed deer. • Two blacker-tailed subspecies occur along the B.C. coast: the "Sitka deer" and the "black-tailed deer."
Where found: open coniferous woodlands, grasslands, river valleys; throughout but more common in central and southern B.C.

Moose

Alces alces

Length: 2.5–3 m
Shoulder height: 1.7–2.1 m
Weight: 230–540 kg

Moose are deer, and darn big ones—the world's largest. These impressive beasts have long legs that help them navigate bogs or deep snow. They can run as fast as 55 km/h, swim continuously for several hours, dive to depths of 6 m and remain submerged for up to 1 minute. • Saplings with the tops snapped off and other damaged plants are signs that a moose stopped by for lunch. This animal is a voracious eater—an individual might consume as much as 7250 kg of vegetation annually. **Where found:** coniferous forests, young poplar stands, willows; east of the Coastal Mountains.

Caribou

Rangifer tarandus

Length: 1.4–2.3 m
Shoulder height: 90–170 cm
Weight: 90–110 kg

The seasonal movements of B.C.'s caribou hardly compare to the incredible migrations of their Arctic kin, but many of them travel between mountains and foothill forests every spring and autumn. In general, B.C. caribou populations spend the summer at high elevations to avoid the heat and flies and descend to lower foraging areas for winter. Caribou feed by digging through the snow with their broad hooves to expose lichens, their favourite winter food. In summer, grasses, mosses, sedges and mushrooms are added to their diet. **Where found:** mature coniferous forests, alpine and subalpine meadows in summer; northern B.C. and Rocky Mountains; also Tweedsmuir PP.

Cougar

Puma concolor

Length: 1.5–2.7 m
Shoulder height: 65–80 cm
Weight: 30–90 kg

Cougars are skilled hunters with special-ized teeth and claws for capturing prey; their sharp canines can kill a moose or deer in one lethal bite. • These nocturnal hunters can travel an average of 10 km per night. Historically, cougars were found from northern B.C. east to the Atlantic and south to Patagonia, with a range overlapping that of deer, their favourite prey. With the coming of settlers, cougars were pushed out of most areas except the western moun-tains and adjacent foothills. **Where found:** variety of habitats that provide cover; throughout except extreme northern B.C. **Also known as:** mountain lion.

Canada Lynx

Lynx canadensis

Length: 80–100 cm
Shoulder height: 45–60 cm
Weight: 7–18 kg

Elusive, elegant and generally secretive, the Canada lynx is a well-equipped hunting machine. It has bristle-tipped ears that can detect the slightest sound, large paws that function as snowshoes and swimming paddles and dense pelage to protect against the bitterest cold. The lynx is an excellent climber and often crouches on tree branches, ready to pounce on passing prey. • Lynx populations fluctuate every 7 to 10 years with snowshoe hare numbers. When hares are plentiful, lynx kittens are more likely to survive and reproduce; when there are fewer hares, more kittens starve and the lynx population declines. **Where found:** coniferous forests; east of the Coastal Mountains.

Bobcat

Lynx rufus

Length: 75–125 cm
Shoulder height: 45–55 cm
Weight: 7–13 kg

The bobcat ranges from southern Canada to cen-tral Mexico, the widest distribution of any native cat in North America. The bobcat is not well adapted to deep snow and is replaced by the Canada lynx in the northern part of its range. • These nocturnal hunters occupy a variety of habitats, including deserts, wetlands and, surprisingly, devel-oped areas. • A feline speedster, the bobcat can hit 48 km/h for short bursts. • All bobcats have dark streaks or spots, but their coat varies from yellowish to rusty brown or grey, depending on habitat and season. The similar-looking lynx has longer ear tufts and a longer, black-tipped tail. **Where found:** open forests and brushy areas; central and southern B.C.

Western Spotted Skunk

Spilogale gracilis

Length: 32–58 cm
Weight: 450–900 g

When threatened, the western spotted skunk stamps its feet in alarm or makes short lunges at its perceived attacker, which will pay the smelly price if it ignores the warning. Although this assault is no laughing matter, the posture this small mammal assumes in order to spray is comical—the skunk literally performs a handstand, arches its back so that its backside and tail face forward above its head, and then walks toward its assailant while spraying it. • When not performing such feats of showmanship, this nocturnal skunk feeds mostly on insects, especially grasshoppers and crickets. **Where found:** woodlands, riparian zones, rocky areas, open grasslands or scrublands and farmlands; primarily in and around Vancouver and southward.

Striped Skunk

Mephitis mephitis

Length: 53–76 cm
Weight: 1.9–4.2 kg

Equipped with a noxious spray that can be shot up to 6 m, the striped skunk gives both humans and animals an overpowering reason to avoid it. But come spring, when the mother skunk emerges with her fluffy, 2-toned babies trotting behind her, you may find yourself enjoying her company—from a distance. Skunk families typically den in hollow logs or rock piles in summer then switch to old woodchuck or badger burrows for winter. **Where found:** moist urban and rural habitats, including hardwood groves and agricultural areas; extreme southwest B.C. and east of the Coastal Mountains.

American Marten

Martes americana

Length: 55–65 cm
Weight: 500–1200 g

Much smaller than the similar fisher and mink, the American marten's relatively diminutive size allows it to use woodpecker cavities for dens, which it often does. The marten prefers coniferous forests but also ranges into mixed hardwood forests. Because it is active during the day, the marten is more likely to be seen than other weasels. It feeds mainly on small rodents but also consumes fish, snakes, small birds or eggs, carrion and sometimes berries. • The marten was prized for its soft, luxurious fur. Trapping combined with habitat loss has contributed to the species' decline. **Where found:** mature coniferous forests; throughout.

Fisher

Martes pennanti

Length: 80–110 cm
Weight: 2–5.5 kg

Like all members of the weasel family, the fisher is an aggressive, capable predator. But the fisher is misnamed: although it can swim well, it rarely eats fish, preferring snowshoe hares and other small mammals. The fisher is one of the only animals that regularly kills porcupines, adeptly flipping them to gain access to the soft, unprotected belly region. • Fishers have specially adapted ankle-bones that allow them to rotate their feet and climb down trees headfirst. These reclusive animals prefer intact wilderness and disappear once development begins. **Where found:** dense coniferous and mixedwood forests; throughout the mainland but absent from some southern areas.

Least Weasel

Mustela nivalis

Length: 15–23 cm
Weight: 28–70 g

Woe be unto the hiding vole that has one of these miniscule barbarians charge into its burrow. The least weasel regularly invades holes in search of prey, and it eats up to its weight in food each day to fuel its incredibly fast metabolism. This small, mainly nocturnal carnivore is rarely seen, but you may glimpse one dashing for cover when you move a hay bale or piece of plywood. • Unlike the larger weasels, the least weasel has a much shorter tail with no black tip. **Where found:** open fields, forest edges, rock piles, abandoned buildings; central and northern B.C.

Short-tailed Weasel

Mustela erminea

Length: 25–33 cm
Weight: 45–105 g

If short-tailed weasels were the size of black bears, we'd all be dead. These voracious, mainly nocturnal predators tend to kill anything they can take down, especially mice and voles. A typical glimpse is of a small, eel-like mammal bounding along then vanishing before a positive ID can be made. • The short-tailed weasel's coat becomes white in winter, but the tail is black-tipped year-round. **Where found:** dense coniferous and mixed forests, shrub lands, meadows and riparian areas; throughout. **Also known as:** ermine, stoat.

Long-tailed Weasel

Mustela frenata

Length: 30–45 cm
Weight: 85–400 g

Like other mustelids, long-tailed weasels exhibit serial-killer tendencies, killing more than they can consume. Excess prey is sometimes cached for later use. These hyperactive beasts are capable hunters that can bring down prey twice their size, though their normal fare consists of small vertebrates, insects and, occasionally, fruit. • Like other true weasels, the long-tailed turns white in winter, but the tip of the tail remains black. **Where found:** open grassy meadows, brushland, woodlots, forest edges, fencerows; central and southern B.C.

American Mink

Neovison vison

Length: 45–70 cm
Weight: 600–1400 g

Because mink were once coveted for their silky fur, over trapping led to localized declines of mink populations. Today, most mink coats are made from ranch-raised animals. • Mink move with graceful, fluid motions, resembling ribbons as they wind along the shorelines. Rarely found far from water, the mink has webbed feet, making it an excellent swimmer and diver that often hunts for underwater prey. Its thick, dark brown to blackish, oily fur insulates the body from extremely cold waters. • Mink travel along established hunting routes, sometimes resting in a muskrat lodge after eating the original inhabitant. **Where found:** shorelines of lakes, marshes, streams; throughout.

Wolverine

Gulo gulo

Length: 70–110 cm
Weight: 7–16 kg

From afar, a wolverine can look like a small brown bear, until its long, bushy tail and golden sides are revealed. This muscular animal is capable of taking down a caribou or moose, but it usually scavenges carrion left behind by larger predators. With its powerful jaws, the wolverine can crunch through bone to access the nourishing marrow, leaving little trace of a carcass. It also eats small animals, fish, bird eggs and berries. With a fondness for plastic and for marking landmarks with musk and urine, a wolverine can wreak havoc on unoccupied exploration camps. • Chances of seeing this elusive animal are slim, even in the most remote areas. **Where found:** throughout mainland.

Badger

Taxidea taxus

Length: 65–90 cm
Weight: 5–11 kg

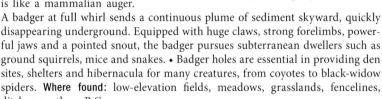

This burly, burrowing beast
is like a mammalian auger.
A badger at full whirl sends a continuous plume of sediment skyward, quickly
disappearing underground. Equipped with huge claws, strong forelimbs, powerful jaws and a pointed snout, the badger pursues subterranean dwellers such as
ground squirrels, mice and snakes. • Badger holes are essential in providing den
sites, shelters and hibernacula for many creatures, from coyotes to black-widow
spiders. **Where found:** low-elevation fields, meadows, grasslands, fencelines,
ditches; southern B.C.

Northern River Otter

Lontra canadensis

Length: 90–140 cm
Weight: 5–11 kg

Playful otters are very entertaining,
whether you are watching them at the
zoo or are lucky enough to see them
in the wild. Their long, streamlined
bodies, fully webbed feet and muscular tails make them swift,
effortless swimmers with incredible fishing ability. • River otters
are highly social animals, usually travelling in small groups. Good clues to their
presence are "slides" on the shores of water bodies or troughs in the snow created
by tobogganing otters. **Where found:** near lakes, ponds, streams; throughout.

Sea Otter

Enhydra lutris

Length: 80–150 cm
Weight: 23–45 kg

This buoyant otter lolls
about on its back like a sun-
bather, floating in a manner humans
can only wish for, even in the saltiest of seas. It can even
sleep on the water after anchoring itself in kelp beds, which are habitat for sea
urchins, this otter's favoured prey. Reluctant to abandon the comfortable recline,
the sea otter grooms itself and dines while floating on its back, using tools such as
rocks to crack open the shells of its prey. **Where found:** shallow coastal areas with
abundant kelp beds; scattered populations along the West Coast.

Black Bear

Ursus americanus

Length: 1.4–1.8 m
Shoulder height: 90–110 cm
Weight: 40–270 kg

Don't be fooled by the black bear's clumsy, lumbering gait—this bear can hit 50 km/h for short bursts. It is also an excellent swimmer and can climb trees. • The black bear is omnivorous, eating an incredibly varied diet and exploiting whatever food source is at hand. During much of the year, up to 3/4 of its diet may be vegetable matter. • One of the few North American mammals that truly hibernates, the black bear packs on the fat, then retires to a sheltered den for winter. • B.C.'s central and north coasts are home to the Kermode or spirit bear, a black bear with white fur. White fur is a rare genetic trait, but the spirit bear is not albino, as it has a brown (not pink) nose and eyes. **Where found:** forests and open, marshy woodlands; throughout.

Grizzly Bear

Ursus arctos

Length: 1.8–2.6 m
Shoulder height: 90–120 cm
Weight: 110–530 kg

Knowing that grizzly bears are around, though they are rarely seen, makes camping in the woods a truly wild experience. A mother grizzly with cubs can be very dangerous; hikers are advised to practice bear avoidance techniques. • Grizzlies have a prominent shoulder hump, a dished face, a pale yellow to dark brown pelage and long front claws, which are always visible. Plants and carrion make up most of their omnivorous diet. **Where found:** forests and riparian areas in valley bottoms to high alpine tundra; throughout mainland except southwestern B.C. **Also known as:** brown bear.

Coyote

Canis latrans

Length: 1–1.3 m
Shoulder height: 58–66 cm
Weight: 10–22 kg

Occasionally forming loose packs and joining in spirited yipping choruses, coyotes are clever and versatile hunter-scavengers. They often range into suburbia and even live in densely populated cities. This dog-like mammal has benefited from large-scale habitat changes, booming in numbers and greatly expanding its range. Widespread eradication of predators such as grey wolves has also helped coyotes flourish. • The coyote has a smaller, thinner muzzle than the wolf, and its tail drags behind its legs when it runs. **Where found:** open woodlands, agricultural lands, near urban areas; throughout mainland.

Grey Wolf

Canis lupus

Length: 1.5–2 m
Shoulder height: 66–97 cm
Weight: 38–54 kg

Wolves have been persecuted since the first Europeans landed in North America and have been eradicated from vast areas of their former range. The animals' large size, fierce predatory behaviour, pack-forming habits and the role they play in fables such as Little Red Riding Hood have instilled fear in many people. Today, wolves in British Columbia are valued symbols of the wilderness and are crucial to a healthy, balanced food chain. • Wolf packs co-operate within a strong social structure that is dominated by an alpha pair (dominant male and female). **Where found:** forests and riparian areas; throughout mainland. **Also known as:** timber wolf.

Red Fox

Vulpes vulpes

Length: 90–110 cm
Shoulder height: 38 cm
Weight: 3.6–6.8 kg

Most red foxes are a rusty, reddish brown, but rare variations include blackish forms and even a silvery type. These small animals look like dogs but often act like cats: they stalk mice and other small prey and make energetic pounces to capture victims. • Dens are typically in old woodchuck burrows or similar holes. Tracks are often the best sign foxes are present: their small, oval prints form a nearly straight line. **Where found:** open habitats with brushy shelter, riparian areas, edge habitats; throughout, east of the Coastal Mountains.

Raccoon

Procyon lotor

Length: 65–100 cm
Weight: 5–14 kg

These black-masked bandits are common in many habitats, including suburbia, and are often found near water. When on the move, raccoons present a hunch-backed appearance and run with a comical, mincing gait. Although they are not true hibernators, they become sluggish during colder weather and may hole up for extended periods. These agile climbers are often seen high in trees or peeking from arboreal cavities. • Raccoons are known for wetting their food before eating, a behaviour that allows them to feel for and discard inedible matter. **Where found:** wooded areas near water; southwestern B.C. and the Queen Charlottes.

Porcupine

Erethizon dorsatum

Length: 66–100 cm
Weight: 3.5–18 kg

Prickly porcupines are best left alone. Contrary to popular myth, they cannot throw their 30,000 or so quills, but with a lightning-fast flick of the tail, they'll readily impale some of their spikes into persistent attackers. • Slow but excellent climbers, porcupines clamber about trees, stripping off the bark and feeding on the sugary cambium layer. Although they are sure-footed, they aren't infallible; in one study, about one-third of museum specimen skeletons examined had old fractures, presumably from arboreal mishaps. • Porcupines crave salt and will gnaw on rubber tires, wooden axe handles, toilet seats and even hiking boots! **Where found:** coniferous and deciduous forests; throughout mainland.

Western Jumping Mouse

Zapus princeps

Length: 22–26 cm
Weight: 15–35 g

Like tiny kangaroos, jumping mice can leap almost 1 m
when startled. They have large hind feet, powerful rear legs
and a long tail to help them balance as they jump. Mostly found in damp
meadows, they can be identified by their distinctive mode of locomotion.
• Western jumping mice hibernate for 6–7 months in underground burrows, one
of the longest periods of any North American mammal. Their metabolism slows
and they survive on stored fat deposits. • The meadow jumping mouse (*Z. hudson-
ius*) is common in central and northern B.C. **Where found:** prefers fields; also forest
edges, marshes, streambanks; throughout.

Bushy-tailed Woodrat

Neotoma cinerea

Length: 28–45 cm (tail 11–23 cm)
Weight: 85–500 g

Woodrats are infamous for
collecting objects, whether
natural or man-made and whether useful or merely decorative accents, for their
large, messy nests. Twigs, bones, pinecones, bottle caps, rings, pens and coins are
picked up as this rodent scouts for treasures, often trading an object in its mouth
for the next, more attractive item it encounters. A woodrat's nest is often more
easily found than the woodrat itself. **Where found:** rocky outcroppings, shrublands, caves and mine shafts; from grasslands to alpine zones; throughout except
offshore islands and northeast B.C. **Also known as:** packrat, trade rat.

Black Rat

Rattus rattus

Length: 33–46 cm
Weight: 120–340 g

The black rat is a more common stowaway
on ships than the brown rat, so it is con-
tinually reintroduced at seaports such as
Vancouver and Victoria. It lives in a wild
state on Vancouver Is. and the Queen Charlotte Is.,
where it is abundant. In B.C. it breeds during the
warmer months and gives birth to 2–8 young. **Where found:** in and around human
structures; extreme southwestern B.C. and the Queen Charlottes

Brown Rat

Rattus norvegicus

Length: 30–46 cm
Weight: 200–480 g

The mammalian counterpart to house sparrows, these introduced rats thrive around human settlements. Native to Europe and Asia—but not Norway—the brown rat came to North America stowed away on early ships. • Brown rats can carry parasites and diseases transferable to wildlife, humans and pets, but captive-bred rats have given psychologists many insights into human learning and behaviour. • Wild brown rats have a brown to reddish brown, often grizzled pelage with grey tones and grey undersides. **Where found:** urban areas, farmyards, garbage dumps; coastal B.C. **Also known as:** Norway rat, common rat, sewer rat, water rat.

House Mouse

Mus musculus

Length: 14–19 cm
Weight: 14–25 g

Chances are if you have a mouse in your house, it is a house mouse. This species has been fraternizing with humans for several thousand years. Like the brown rat, it stowed away on ships from Europe, quickly spreading across North America with settlers. • House mice are gregarious and social, even grooming one another. They are destructive in dwellings, however, shredding insulation for nests, leaving droppings and raiding pantries. • These tiny beasts have brownish to blackish grey backs and grey undersides. **Where found:** usually associated with human settlements, including houses, garages, farms, garbage dumps, granaries; throughout.

Deer Mouse

Peromyscus maniculatus

Length: 12–18 cm
Weight: 18–35 g

This abundant mouse often occupies cavities in trees, stumps and logs, old buildings and bluebird nest boxes, where it builds a dense nest of plant matter. These little critters are strong swimmers, and they often brave the water to colonize islands. They primarily eat nuts, berries, seeds, vegetation and insects, but will also raid your pantry. **Where found:** various habitats,0 including woodlands, riparian areas, shrubby areas, some farmlands; throughout except central and north coast.

Southern Red-backed Vole

Clethrionomys gapperi

Length: 12–16 cm
Weight: 12–43 g

Active day and night in spruce-fir forests and bogs, this
abundant vole is easily recognized by its reddish-brown
back on an otherwise greyish body. As with other voles, the southern red-backed
vole does not hibernate during winter; instead, it tunnels through the subnivean
layer—along the ground, under the snow—in search of seeds, nuts and leaves.
• Populations of these prolific voles vary according to predators and food supplies.
They are probably the primary prey of the northern saw-whet owl. **Where found:**
mixed and coniferous forests, bogs, riparian areas; throughout except northwestern B.C., where it is replaced by the northern red-backed vole (*C. rutilus*).

Meadow Vole

Microtus pennsylvanicus

Length: 14–20 cm
Weight: 18–64 g

Meadow voles rank high among the world's most
prolific breeders. If unchecked by predators, they
would practically rule the earth. • Little furry sau-
sages with legs, meadow voles are important food for raptors, especially in winter.
Their populations have cyclical highs and lows, and in boom years impressive
numbers of hawks and owls will congregate in good vole fields. Primarily active
at night, this common vole can be seen during the day as well, especially when
populations are high. **Where found:** open woodlands, meadows, fields, fencelines,
marshes; throughout.

Long-tailed Vole

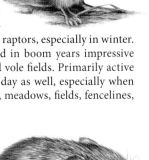

Microtus longicaudus

Length: 17–23 cm
Weight: 35–57 g

Long-tailed voles thrive above the
treeline in mountain parks, but also
live on grasslands, wet meadows and
thickets. Unlike meadow voles, this species does not follow distinct tunnel-like
paths through the grass, but instead ranges widely at night. Some research suggests that birds of prey can actually see the glow of vole urine owing to chemicals
that reflect in the ultra-violet range. Thus, raptors can quickly discern where voles
are. Long-tailed voles feed mainly on green leaves, grasses, fruit and tree bark.
Where found: variety of habitats; throughout mainland.

Northern Bog Lemming

Synaptomys borealis

Length: 11–14 cm
Weight: 27–35 g

Lemmings look rather like voles but have larger, rounded heads. They live primarily in extensive systems of subsurface tunnels and feed mainly on grasses and sedges. Neatly clipped piles of grass along paths and their curious green scat indicate northern bog lemmings are nearby. Lemmings remain active during winter, tunnelling through the subnivean layer—along the ground, under the snow. • Populations can vary from year to year, and in boom years especially, they are a major prey item for predators. **Where found:** burrows among sedges and grasses, moist spruce forests, sphagnum bogs; throughout mainland.

Muskrat

Ondatra zibethicus

Length: 15–60 cm
Weight: 800–1600 g

More comfortable in water than on land, the muskrat has a laterally compressed tail that allows it to swim like a fish. Its occurrence in wetlands is easily detected by the presence of cone-shaped lodges made from cattails and other vegetation. • Muskrats play an important role in marsh management by thinning out dense stands of cattails. They also vex marsh managers by digging burrows in dikes. In general, muskrats are quite valuable in wetland ecosystems, creating diversified habitats that benefit many other species. **Where found:** lakes, marshes, ponds, rivers, reservoirs, dugouts, canals; throughout.

Beaver

Castor canadensis

Length: 90–120 cm
Weight: 16–30 kg

No mammal influences its environment to the degree that this jumbo rodent—North America's largest—does. Its complex dams are engineering marvels that create ponds and wetlands for a diversity of flora and fauna. The presence of conical, gnawed stubs of tree trunks is a sure sign a beaver is present. With a loud warning slap of its tail on water, the beaver often disappears before it is detected. • Beavers were nearly exterminated in many areas at one time, trapped prolifically for their valuable pelts. They have made an amazing comeback and are once again common. **Where found:** lakes, ponds, marshes, slow-flowing rivers and streams; throughout.

Mountain Beaver

Aplodontia rufa

Length: 30–47 cm
Weight: 300–1400 g

Capable of swimming only short distances, this rodent prefers to climb trees, and rather than build an aquatic den, it burrows tunnels and nesting chambers into dry ground. • The mountain beaver feeds primarily on sword ferns and bracken ferns, which are toxic to most other rodents, but also forages on seedlings and the cambium of saplings; the male eats large amounts of red alder leaves in fall. **Where found:** deciduous forests with plenty of shrubs, forbs and young trees; from near sea level to the treeline; Hope/Princeton area, especially Manning PP.

Woodchuck

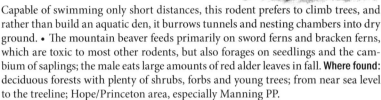

Marmota monax

Length: 46–66 cm
Weight: 1.8–5.4 kg

Burly woodchucks have powerful claws for digging burrows up to 15 m long. Most people are used to seeing woodchucks scuttling along on the ground, so it is a surprise to find them high up a tree, but they are squirrels, after all. More typically, they graze along forest edges and clearings, using their sharp incisors to rapidly cut plants, bark and berries. • Woodchucks are true hibernators and spend much of the year tucked away underground. Groundhog Day (February 2) celebrates their emergence. **Where found:** meadows, pastures, open woodlands; central and northern areas. **Also known as:** groundhog.

Hoary Marmot

Marmota caligata

Length: 50–80 cm
Weight: 5–9 kg

High in alpine environments, hoary marmots excavate burrows under rocky terrain to hide from the elements and from predators such as eagles and foxes. They greet alpine hikers with a shrill whistle, from which the marmot's old nickname "whistler" is derived. • Marmots spend their lazy days eating, sleeping and raising young, basking in the summer sun or hibernating in winter. • The yellow-bellied marmot (*M. flaventris*) is found in central B.C. and the rare Vancouver Island marmot (*M. vancouverensis*) is endemic to Vancouver Is. **Where found:** rocky, alpine tundra and subalpine areas near abundant vegetation; throughout northern B.C., Coastal and Rocky mountains.

Columbian Ground Squirrel

Spermophilus columbianus

Length: 33–41 cm
Weight: 350–800 g

This vocal beast is sometimes heard before it is seen. Robust Columbian ground squirrels chirp loudly, often at the first sight of anything unusual, and issue loud trills. These common ground squirrels are found everywhere from montane valleys to alpine meadows. • Columbian ground squirrels have been known to hibernate for up to 220 days. Some authorities believe they spend up to 90% of their lives underground. **Where found:** various habitats, primarily meadows and grassy areas; also woodlands, alpine tundra; east-central B.C. and southward.

Golden-mantled Ground Squirrel

Spermophilus lateralis

Length: 28–33 cm
Weight: 170–340 g

A familiar campground resident, this ground squirrel is frequently referred to as a large chipmunk because of somewhat similar striping. Closer inspection reveals a distinct difference: the stripes stop short of this ground squirrel's neck; all chipmunks have stripes running through their cheeks. The golden-mantled ground squirrel often has its cheek pouches crammed with seeds. **Where found:** montane and subalpine forests with rocky outcroppings or talus slopes; east-central B.C and southward.

Yellow-pine Chipmunk

Tamias amoenus

Length: 20–24 cm
Weight: 45–85 g

This cute, curious rodent is often the most commonly seen chipmunk in B.C. Its habitat ranges from sagebrush flats to coniferous forests, and it plays an important role in forest ecology. In addition to hoarding food in its burrow, the yellow-pine chipmunk often "loses" nuts and other fruit, helping to distribute plants. • Although chipmunks more or less hibernate from autumn until spring, they wake every few weeks to feed, even coming above ground in mild weather. • The least chipmunk (*T. minimus*) replaces the yellow-pine chipmunk in northern B.C. **Where found:** various habitats, campgrounds; central and southern areas.

Red Squirrel

Tamiasciurus hudsonicus

Length: 28–34 cm
Weight: 140–250 g

This pugnacious and vocal squirrel often drives
larger squirrels and birds from bird feeders, and
sometimes takes bird eggs and nestlings. It can eat
highly poisonous *Amanita* mushrooms and will
bite into sugar maple bark to feed on sap. Large mid-
dens of discarded pinecone scales are evidence of its buried
food bounty. • The red squirrel may chatter, stomp its feet, flick its tail and scold
you with a piercing cry. • During the short spring courtship, squirrels engage in
incredibly acrobatic chases. **Where found:** coniferous and mixed forests; throughout.

Eastern Grey Squirrel

Sciurus carolinensis

Length: 43–50 cm
Weight: 400–710 g

Through much of the Lower Mainland and southeastern Vancouver Is.,
this large, introduced tree squirrel's antics enter-
tain park visitors and urban residents. Although
called grey squirrel after the colour form common
in its eastern range, most of the squirrels in B.C. are black. Originally a species of
large, mature forests, grey squirrels now thrive in suburbia. Their large, roundish
nests are conspicuous in trees, but their winter den sites and birthing locales are in
tree cavities. **Where found:** mature deciduous or mixed forests with nut-bearing trees;
extreme southwestern B.C. **Also known as:** black squirrel.

Northern Flying Squirrel

Glaucomys sabrinus

Length: 24–36 cm
Weight: 75–180 g

Long flaps of skin (called the "patagium") stretched between the fore and hind limbs
and a broad, flattened tail allow this nocturnal flying squirrel to glide swiftly from tree
to tree. After landing, the squirrel inevitably hustles around to the opposite side of the
trunk in case a predator, such as an owl, has followed. • The flying squirrel plays an
important role in forest ecology because it digs up and eats truffles, the fruiting bodies
of ectomycorrhizal fungus that grows underground. Through its stool, the squirrel
spreads the beneficial fungus, helping both the fungus and the forest plants. **Where
found:** primarily old-growth coniferous and mixed forests; throughout mainland.

73

Snowshoe Hare

Lepus americanus

Length: 38–53 cm
Weight: 1–1.5 kg

Snowshoe hares are completely adapted for life in snowy conditions. Large, snowshoe-like feet enable them to traverse powdery snow without sinking. Primarily nocturnal, they blend perfectly with their surroundings regardless of the season. They are greyish, reddish or blackish brown in summer, and white in winter. • If detected, the hare explodes into a running zigzag pattern in its flight for cover, reaching speeds of up to 50 km/h on hard-packed snow trails. **Where found:** brushy or forested areas; throughout mainland.

Mountain Cottontail

Sylvilagus nuttallii

Length: 34–40 cm
Weight: 700–1000 g

The mountain cottontail is our smallest member of the rabbit family. • Adapted to the arid grasslands, and found only in the Okanagan region, the cottontail avoids daytime predators by hiding under rocks, machinery or in dugout depressions under thorny shrubs. It emerges at dusk to graze on grasses and forbs, sagebrush or juniper berries, but the cottontail never strays far from cover. • The introduced eastern cottontail (*S. floridanus*) has pale, buffy grey pelage and cinnamon neck and leg markings and is found in the Fraser River delta and southeastern Vancouver Is. **Where found:** variety of habitats near shrubby cover; Okanagan region of B.C. **Also known as:** Nuttall's cottontail.

European Rabbit

Oryctolagus cuniculus

Length: 45–60 cm
Weight: 1.4–2.3 kg

The European rabbit is the forerunner of all domestic rabbits. As with the domestic dog, there are hundreds of rabbit breeds and varieties. Coat colour is highly variable and may be an array of greys or browns, black and white, or multicoloured. These introduced rabbits are well naturalized on southeastern Vancouver Is., particularly on the University of Victoria campus and the Victoria General Hospital. **Where found:** open fields, brushy areas and parkland; southeastern Vancouver Is.

Pika

Ochotona princeps

Length: 16–21 cm
Weight: 150–300 g

The busy pika scurries in and out of rocky crevices
to issue its warning *PEEEK!* call and to gather large
bundles of succulent grasses to dry on sun-drenched rocks and store for later con-
sumption during winter, when it rarely leaves its shelter under the snow. In summer, it makes grassy nests within the rocks to have its young. • Although tailless
and with rounded ears, the pika is a close relative of rabbits and hares. **Where
found:** rocky talus slopes and rocky fields at higher elevations; southern B.C.

Masked Shrew

Sorex cinereus

Length: 7–11 cm
Weight: 2–7 g

This mammal is one of our most abundant—but good luck seeing one. Mostly
nocturnal and prone to scurrying about in dense cover, this voracious shrew
consumes its body weight or more in food daily. To balance high late-winter mor-
tality rates and year-round predation, a female may have 2 to 3 litters per year,
giving birth to as many as 8 blind, toothless and naked young at a time. • The
northern water shrew (*S. palustris*) has a black back and silver underparts and is
also common throughout the mainland and Vancouver Is. **Where found:** forests,
occasionally tall-grass prairies; throughout mainland. **Also known as:** cinereus shrew.

Pygmy Shrew

Sorex hoyi

Length: 5–6 cm
Weight: 2–7 g

The pygmy shrew is our smallest mam-
mal and weighs no more than a penny. • This pennyweight shrew stands up on its
hind legs, curiously like a bear. • Because of its size and secretive habits, the
pygmy shrew is seldom observed, at least not well enough to be identified. •
Shrews have an incredibly high metabolic rate, with heart rates often reaching
1200 beats per minute. Most of the heat energy they produce is quickly lost, so
pygmy shrews routinely eat 3 times their body weight in a day, taking down and
consuming any prey that can be overpowered. **Where found:** various habitats, from
forests to open fields, sphagnum bogs; east of the Coastal Mountains.

Virginia Opossum

Didelphis virginiana

Length: 69–84 cm
Weight: 1.1–1.6 kg

A maternal pouch, opposable "thumbs" and a scaly, prehensile tail characterize the opossum. The only marsupial north of Mexico also has more teeth—50—than any of our other mammals. Honeybee-sized babies are born out of the pouch and must find their way into its folds immediately after birth. • Opossums are most famous for feigning death or "playing possum" when attacked. Because they scavenge on road kill, they too often become victims. • Opossums do not hibernate, and their bare ears and tails are vulnerable to frostbite—they commonly lose parts of their extremities. **Where found:** agricultural lands; extreme southwestern B.C. (Lower Mainland).

Long-eared Bat

Myotis evotis

Length: 8.3–11 cm
Forearm length: 3.8–4.1 cm
Weight: 3.5–8.9 g

With Spock-like ears, the long-eared bat presents an outrageous visage—if you are lucky enough to admire one close up. • Most bats forage by catching insects while in flight, pursuing them with incredible aerial acrobatics. Instead, the long-eared bat picks its insect victim from the foliage of trees then hangs from a branch to consume it. • With almost 1000 species found worldwide, bats are the most successful mammals next to rodents. **Where found:** forested areas; roosts in tree cavities, under peeling bark, in rock crevices; hibernates in caves, abandoned mines; southern B.C.

Little Brown Bat

Myotis lucifugus

Length: 7–10 cm
Forearm Length: 3.5–4 cm
Weight: 5.3–9 g

Each spring, these bats form maternal roosting colonies that can number thousands of individuals—one colony had nearly 7000 bats. Virtually helpless at birth, the single offspring clings to its mother's chest until it is strong enough to remain at the roost site. • A single little brown bat can consume 900 insects per hour. This species is probably the most common bat in the region and is the most likely to be seen at dusk. **Where found:** roosts in buildings, barns, caves, crevices, hollow trees, under tree bark; hibernates in buildings, caves, old mines; throughout.

Hoary Bat

Lasiurus cinereus

Length: 11–15 cm
Forearm Length: 4.5–5.7 cm
Weight: 19–35 g

Hoary bats are the most widely distributed—and arguably the most beautiful—bats in North America. Their large size and frosty silver fur make them quite distinctive. Identify them at night by their size and slow wingbeats over open terrain. • These bats roost in trees, not caves or buildings, and wrap their wings around themselves for protection against the elements. They often roost in orchards, but they are insectivores and do no damage to fruit crops. **Where found:** roosts on branches of coniferous and deciduous trees, occasionally in tree cavities; migrates south for winter; southern B.C.

Silver-haired Bat

Lasionycteris noctivagans

Length: 9–11 cm
Forearm Length: 3.8–4.5 cm
Weight: 7–18 g

Silver-haired bats are most likely to be found roosting under a loose piece of bark. Sometimes they occur in small, loosely associated groups. • These bats mate in autumn, but actual fertilization doesn't occur until spring. This odd strategy ensures that plenty of food will be available when their young are born. • To conserve energy on cold days, they can lower their body temperature and metabolism, a state known as torpor. • This bat's black flight membrane can span 30 cm. **Where found:** roosts in cavities and crevices of old-growth trees; migrates south for winter; throughout except extreme northern B.C.

Big Brown Bat

Eptesicus fuscus

Length: 9–14 cm
Forearm Length: 4.6–5.4 cm
Weight: 12–28 g

This bat's ultrasonic echolocation (20,000 to 110,000 Hz) can detect flying beetles and moths up to 5 m away. It flies above water or around streetlights searching for prey, which it scoops up with its wing and tail membranes. • Few animals rest as much as bats, and they can live for many decades as a result of the low stresses on their physiological systems. After spending 2 or 3 hours on the wing each evening, they perch and their body functions slow down for the rest of the day. **Where found:** in and around artificial structures, occasionally roosting in hollow trees, rock crevices; hibernates in caves, mines, old buildings; central and southern B.C.

BIRDS

Birds are the most diverse class of vertebrates. All birds are feathered but not all fly. Traits common to all birds are that they are 2-legged, warm-blooded and lay hard-shelled eggs. Some migrate south in the colder winter months and return north in spring. For this reason, the bird diversity of British Columbia varies with the seasons. Some of our well-known winter birds include chickadees, downy woodpeckers, waxwings, nuthatches and snowy owls. Spring brings scores of migrant waterfowl and colourful songbirds that breed in the region and other birds such as shorebirds that continue on to arctic breeding grounds. Even more migratory birds pass through in autumn, their numbers bolstered by young of the year. Many are in duller plumage at this time, and they are largely silent. Scores of migrating birds fly as far south as Central and South America. These neotropical migrants are of concern to biologists and conservationists because habitat degradation and loss, collisions with human-made towers, pesticide use and other factors threaten the birds' survival. Education and increasing appreciation for wildlife may encourage solutions to these problems.

Waterfowl
pp. 80–84

Grouse-like Birds
p. 84

Diving Birds
pp. 85–87

Herons & Vultures
p. 87

Birds of Prey
pp. 88–90

Rails & Cranes
pp. 90–91

Shorebirds
pp. 91–94

Gulls, Terns & Alcids
pp. 95–97

Pigeons
p. 97

Owls
p. 98

Nighthawks & Swifts
p. 99

Hummingbirds & Kingfishers
pp. 99–100

Woodpeckers
pp. 100–01

Flycatchers
pp. 101–02

Shrikes & Vireos
p. 102

Jays & Crows
pp. 103–04

Larks & Swallows
pp. 104–05

Chickadees & Nuthatches
pp. 105–06

Wrens, Dippers & Kinglets
p. 107

Bluebirds & Thrushes
p. 108

Starlings & Waxwings
p. 109

Wood-warblers & Tanagers
pp. 109–11

Sparrows & Grosbeaks
pp. 111–12

Blackbirds & Allies
p. 113

Finch-like Birds
p. 114

Snow Goose

Chen caerulescens

Length: 71–84 cm
Wingspan: 1.4–1.5 m

Noisy flocks of snow geese fly in wavy, disorganized lines, and individuals give a loud, nasal *houk-houk* in flight, higher pitched and more constant than Canada geese. Snow geese breed in the Arctic, some travelling as far as northeastern Siberia and crossing the Bering Strait twice a year. These common geese have all-white bodies and black wing tips. An equally common colour morph, the "blue goose" has a dark body and white head, and was considered a distinct species until 1983. **Where found:** croplands, fields, marshes; common Sept–Mar along the coast; rare elsewhere.

Canada Goose

Branta canadensis

Length: 90–120 cm
Wingspan: up to 1.8 m

Few avian spectacles rival that of immense flocks of migratory Canada geese. The collective honking of airborne groups can be heard for 2 km or more. • A pair of Canada geese will remain together for life, each year raising, teaching and aggressively defending 2–11 young. • In 2004, the Canada goose was split into 2 species—the larger Canada goose, and the smaller, mallard-sized cackling goose (*B. hutchinsii*). Cacklers often travel with migrating Canada geese, but many winter with their own type in the southern U.S. **Where found:** lakeshores, riverbanks, ponds, farmlands, city parks; common summer resident throughout; year-round in south.

Tundra Swan

Cygnus columbianus

Length: 1.2–1.5 m
Wingspan: 1.8–2.1 m

As waters begin to thaw in early April, noisy tundra swans arrive in our southern prairies to feed in flooded agricultural fields and pastures. Swans have all-white wings, unlike snow geese, which have black wing tips. • Other than the rare trumpeter swan, this species is the largest native bird in our region—adults can weigh 7 kg. It would take about 2075 hummingbirds to equal the weight of a tundra swan, illustrating the dramatic diversity of the bird world. **Where found:** shallow areas of lakes and wetlands, flooded agricultural fields, pastures; locally common in Interior during migration and winter; locally uncommon on coast, Nov–Mar.

Wood Duck

Aix sponsa

Length: 38–50 cm
Wingspan: 76 cm

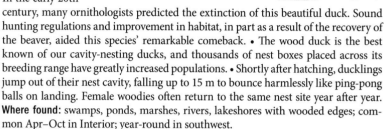

In the early 20th
century, many ornithologists predicted the extinction of this beautiful duck. Sound
hunting regulations and improvement in habitat, in part as a result of the recovery of
the beaver, aided this species' remarkable comeback. • The wood duck is the best
known of our cavity-nesting ducks, and thousands of nest boxes placed across its
breeding range have greatly increased populations. • Shortly after hatching, ducklings
jump out of their nest cavity, falling up to 15 m to bounce harmlessly like ping-pong
balls on landing. Female woodies often return to the same nest site year after year.
Where found: swamps, ponds, marshes, rivers, lakeshores with wooded edges; common Apr–Oct in Interior; year-round in southwest.

Mallard

Anas platyrhynchos

Length: 51–71 cm
Wingspan: 76 cm

The male mallard, with its shiny green
head, chestnut brown breast and stereotypi-
cal quack, is one of the best-known and most
commonly seen ducks. • Mallards are
extremely adaptable and become semi-tame
fixtures on suburban ponds. They remain
year-round wherever open water is available.
• After breeding, male ducks lose their elaborate plumage, helping them
stay camouflaged during their flightless period. In early autumn, they moult back
into breeding colours. **Where found:** almost any large or small wetland; common
throughout, Mar–Nov; year-round in south.

Northern Pintail

Anas acuta

Length: *Male:* 64–76 cm;
Female: 51–56 cm
Wingspan: 86 cm

The beautiful northern pintail is elegant and graceful both
on water and in the air. The male's 2 long, pointed tail feathers are easily seen in
flight and point skyward when the bird tips up to dabble. • Northern pintails are
the most widely distributed duck in the world. Despite impressive numbers in our
region, drought, wetland drainage and changing agricultural practices are the
most serious threats contributing to a slow population decline. **Where found:** shallow wetlands, flooded fields, lake edges; common east of Coastal Mountains,
Mar–Nov; overwinters along coast.

Green-winged Teal

Anas crecca

Length: 30–41 cm
Wingspan: 51–58 cm

Green-winged teals, at only 0.5 kg, are the smallest of our dabbling ducks. They are among the most widely hunted ducks and choose secluded breeding grounds. After breeding, males often undergo a partial migration before moulting into duller "eclipse" plumage. These teals lose all of their flight feathers at once, rendering them flightless for a few weeks, during which they must avoid predators by hiding in thick vegetation or roosting in open water. **Where found:** various freshwater and estuarine habitats, favouring shallow marshes with low cover; common throughout, Mar–Nov; overwinters along coast.

Redhead

Aythya americana

Length: 46–56 cm
Wingspan: 66–74 cm

During the breeding season, redhead pairs favour the south-central Interior, choosing habitats with plenty of skirting emergent vegetation and lush bottom growth for foraging. • During winter, redheads prefer large lakes, and unlike most ducks, the largest numbers occur in the Interior, not on coast. • The best way to separate redheads and similar canvasbacks *(A. valisineria)* is by head shape. The redhead has a round head that meets the bill at an angle; the canvasback has a sloping head that seems to merge with the bill. **Where found:** freshwater wetlands in summer; larger lakes in winter; common in Interior, Mar–Nov.

Lesser Scaup

Aythya affinis

Length: 38–45 cm
Wingspan: 63 cm

Like an Oreo cookie, scaups are white in the middle and dark at both ends. Two similar-looking species occur in our region, the lesser and greater scaup *(A. marila)*, but it takes a lot of experience to reliably separate them in the field. • Lesser scaups are the most abundant diving ducks in North America. They make up nearly 90% of the total scaup population, but for unknown reasons, scaup populations—both lesser and greater—are decreasing by more than 150,000 birds per year. **Where found:** usually freshwater habitats; common on southern coast, Nov–Mar; common Mar–Oct in Interior.

Harlequin Duck

Histrionicus histrionicus

Length: 38–46 cm
Wingspan: 64–69 cm

These beautiful ducks are found year-round along the rocky coastline from Haida Gwaii (Queen Charlotte Is.) to the southern tip of Vancouver Is. Major moulting sites include many of the Gulf Is. as well as rocky shores around Greater Victoria. • Ocean waters surging around rocky headlands or clusters of intertidal boulders attract harlequin ducks, and they seem to enjoy the turbulent roar and tumble of the roughest whitewater. **Where found:** shallow, fast-flowing creeks and rivers, Apr–Oct; intertidal areas and rocky coastal shorelines in winter.

Surf Scoter

Melanitta perspicillata

Length: 43–53 cm
Wingspan: 74–79 cm

Scoters are sea ducks with mostly black bodies and brightly coloured, "swollen" bills. • Surf scoters are very common here in winter, but their migration activity forges the strongest impressions. Throughout most of spring, they gather in immense numbers anywhere that Pacific herring are spawning, creating an annual birdwatching spectacle. Offshore, flock after flock may be observed migrating past a given point over the course of several hours, and a thorough scan of the ocean will reveal a slowly wavering line of these birds just above the horizon. **Where found:** abundant in coastal bays and inlets in winter; common migrant on large Interior lakes.

Common Goldeneye

Bucephala clangula

Length: 41–51 cm
Wingspan: 66 cm

Common golden-eyes are sometimes called "whistlers" because the drake's wings create a loud, distinc-tive hum in flight. Goldeneyes in North America spend their entire life breeding in the boreal forests and overwintering along marine coastlines or inland as far north as open water can be found. • In mid-April, testosterone-flooded males begin their crazy courtship dances. Emitting low buzzes, drakes thrust their heads forward, lunge across the water and kick their brilliant orange feet forward like aquatic break-dancers. **Where found:** common in coastal bays and estuaries, Oct–Mar; breeds on freshwater wetlands in central and northern B.C.

Common Merganser

Mergus merganser

Length: 56–69 cm
Wingspan: 86 cm

Drake mergansers ride low in the water. Noticeably larger than most other species of ducks, these jumbos can tip the scales at 1.6 kg, making them one of our heaviest ducks. Mergansers' bills are sharply serrated, like carving knives, and are designed to seize fishy prey. • Outside of the breeding season, mergansers are highly social, forming large flocks. **Where found:** year-round on coast; common, local on large forest-lined rivers, deep lakes or reservoirs in southern ⅔ of B.C., Apr–Oct.

Ring-necked Pheasant

Phasianus colchicus

Length: *Male:* 76–91 cm; *Female:* 51–66 cm
Wingspan: *Male:* 71–84 cm; *Female:* 49–63 cm

The spectacular Asian ring-necked pheasant was introduced to North America in the mid-1800s, mainly for hunting purposes. Unlike most other introduced species, ringnecks became established in southern areas and thrived almost everywhere they were released. The distinctive, loud *krahh-krawk* of the male pheasant is often heard, but the birds themselves are less frequently observed. • Like other game birds, pheasants have poorly developed flight muscles and rarely fly far. **Where found:** farmlands, brushy hedgerows, forest edges and marshes; rarely found in dry areas; locally common year-round in southern B.C.

Ruffed Grouse

Bonasa umbellus

Length: 38–48 cm
Wingspan: 56 cm

A displaying ruffed grouse makes a sound that is felt more than heard. Each spring, the male proclaims his territory by strutting along a fallen log with his tail fanned wide and his neck feathers ruffed, beating the air with accelerating wing strokes. Drumming is primarily restricted to spring, but the ruffed grouse may also drum for a few weeks in autumn. • Ruffed grouse are well adapted to their northern environment. In autumn and early winter, scales on the sides of their toes grow out, creating temporary snowshoes. **Where found:** deciduous and mixed forests, riparian woodlands; undergoes cyclical fluctuations; year-round resident throughout mainland and Vancouver Is.

Common Loon

Gavia immer

Length: 71–89 cm
Wingspan: 1.2–1.5 m

The wild, yodelling cries of
loons are a symbol of northern
wilderness and evoke images of remote lakes. These graceful swimmers have
nearly solid bones that decrease their buoyancy (most birds have hollow bones),
and their feet are placed well back on their bodies to aid in underwater propul-
sion. Small bass, perch and sunfish are all fair game for these excellent underwater hunters that will chase fish to depths of up to 55 m. **Where found:** common on
coastal inlets, harbours, bays, Oct–Mar; common on large lakes, rivers throughout Interior, Apr–Oct.

Red-necked Grebe

Podiceps grisegena

Length: 43–56 cm
Wingspan: 56 cm

nonbreeding

Migrating red-necked grebes
flood into the lakes of eastern B.C.
during late March and early April.
While this species does migrate along
the coast, most birds fly to and from their breeding grounds over land—at night.
Unlike other spots in North America, red-necks are more solitary in winter in
B.C. waters. • Like other grebes, red-necks carry their newly hatched young on
their backs. The young can stay aboard even when the parents dive underwater.
Where found: common migrant, widespread in winter on sheltered coastal waters;
common east of Coastal Mountains on lakes, ponds, Mar–Oct.

Eared Grebe

Podiceps nigricollis

Length: 30–36 cm
Wingspan: 54–58 cm

Eared grebes undergo cyclical periods of atrophy and hypertrophy of
their internal organs and pectoral muscles, depending on whether or not the
birds need to migrate. This strategy leaves
eared grebes flightless for up to 10 months annually—
longer than any other flying bird in the world. • Typically colonial nesters, these
grebes make floating platform nests among thick vegetation on the edge of a lake
or wetland. **Where found:** uncommon on coast; common on wetlands, large lakes
and sewage disposal ponds in central and southern B.C., Apr–Oct.

Sooty Shearwater

Puffinus griseus

Length: 41–46 cm
Wingspan: 1.0 m

Each summer, in numbers beyond estimation, shearwaters of several species arrive off the B.C. coast from breeding islands in the Southern Hemisphere. One of the world's commonest birds, the sooty shearwater dominates the hundreds of thousands of birds spread out on the open ocean. • Sooties have the longest migration of any species, flying 64,000 km from their summer home in New Zealand to rich feeding areas off Alaska and Japan. Any offshore boat trip between May and September will reveal scattered individuals or huge flocks. **Where found:** common to abundant on open ocean, Apr–Oct.

Fork-tailed Storm-Petrel

Oceanodroma furcata

Length: 20–22 cm
Wingspan: 46 cm

The silver-tipped wings and deeply forked tail of this small marine bird are good field marks as it dances just above the ocean's surface searching for food. • A pair of fork-tails will place their single egg at the end of an underground burrow, then the adults maintain a strictly nocturnal schedule involving shift changes and taking turns to feed the nestling out of sight of avian predators. During the day, adults spread out over the open ocean, sometimes travelling hundreds of kilometres in search of food. **Where found:** locally common on open ocean, Apr–Oct.

American White Pelican

Pelecanus erythrorhynchos

Length: 1.3–1.7 m
Wingspan: 3 m

The American white pelican feeds co-operatively, swimming in flocks and herding fish into shallow water. As a pelican lifts its bill from the water, the fish are held within the flexible pouch while the water drains, then the fish are swallowed whole. A pelican's pouch can hold up to 12 L of water! • In B.C., majestic pelicans breed in the Creston-Williams Lake area, but most breeding colonies are located in the Canadian prairies and the western United States. White pelicans winter from the southern U.S. states to Guatemala, travelling between breeding and wintering areas in flocks of dozens of individuals. **Where found:** uncommon to locally common on freshwater lakes and slow-moving rivers of south-central Interior, Apr–Oct.

Double-crested Cormorant

Phalacrocorax auritus

Length: 66–81 cm
Wingspan: 1.3 m

Double-crested cormorants out-swim fish, which they capture in underwater dives. Most water birds have waterproof feathers, but the structure of the cormorant's feathers allows water in. "Wettable" feathers make this bird less buoyant and a better diver. It has sealed nostrils for diving and therefore must occasionally open its bill to breathe while in flight. Cormorants feed mainly on shallow water, non-commercial fish such as suckers. **Where found:** common year-round in coastal waters; breeds on rocky offshore coastal islands and at Stum Lake in Creston Valley.

Great Blue Heron

Ardea herodias

Length: 1.3–1.4 m
Wingspan: 1.8 m

Common and widespread along the coast and across the southern Interior, the great blue heron is probably the best-known bird in British Columbia. It hunts a variety of small animals day or night along rivers, lakeshores, beaches, fields and seashores. • In B.C., most great blue herons nest together in the tops of trees in sites often known as rookeries. The oldest known colony in British Columbia is in Vancouver's Stanley Park, where permanent scopes are set up to view the birds. **Where found:** almost any salt, fresh or brackish waters throughout B.C., year-round in south, Apr–Oct elsewhere.

Turkey Vulture

Cathartes aura

Length: 66–81 cm
Wingspan: 1.7–1.8 m

Turkey vultures rarely flap their wings, and they rock slightly from side to side as they soar. They hold their wings in a V-shaped position. Endowed with incredible vision and olfactory senses, turkey vultures can detect carrion, their only food source, at great distances. • Vultures often form communal roosts in trees, atop buildings, in barn lofts or on power line towers and will use the same roosting sites for decades. Do not approach a nest; turkey vultures vomit a decidedly unpleasant goop on invaders. **Where found:** habitat generalist; southern B.C., Apr–Sept; rare in winter.

Osprey

Pandion haliaetus

Length: 56–64 cm
Wingspan: 1.4–1.8 m

Often called the "fish hawk," ospreys eat fish exclusively, which they capture in dramatic dives from great heights. They have specialized feet for gripping slippery prey—2 toes point forward, 2 point backward and all are covered with sharp spines. • Ospreys build bulky stick nests on high, artificial structures such as communication towers and utility poles, or on buoys in water. Nesting pairs have increased greatly in recent years, as the chemical DDT has gradually disappeared from the environment. That toxin accumulated in fish and greatly reduced osprey reproductive abilities. **Where found:** lakes, rivers, protected coastal bays; common in southern ⅔ of province, Apr–Oct.

Bald Eagle

Haliaeetus leucocephalus

Length: 80–110 cm
Wingspan: 1.7–2.4 m

Thousands of eagles gather at spawning sites to feast on spawned-out salmon each autumn and winter or "herring balls" and other schooling fish in summer. Annual eagle festivals at Brackendale and Harrison Bay celebrate the return of the eagles and afford unparalleled viewing opportunities. • Bald eagles mate for life and can live up to 40 years. An estimated 20–35% of the world's population of bald eagles breed in the province, with the highest concentrations along the coast within 100 m of the shore. **Where found:** breeds near water; forages in various habitats; widespread year-round resident along coast and throughout southern ½ of Interior, Apr–Oct.

Northern Harrier

Circus cyaneus

Length: 40–60 cm
Wingspan: 1.1–1.2 m

A perched northern harrier looks astonishingly like an owl: it has prominent facial discs to better detect and focus sounds. In flight, this graceful raptor is unmistakable. Harriers have a distinctive white rump patch and fly low over the ground on wings held above horizontal. Their sudden appearance startles small prey such as voles, which are quickly pounced on. • Britain's Royal Air Force was so impressed by the northern harrier's maneuverability that it named the Harrier aircraft after this bird. **Where found:** open country, including fields, marshes; locally common in Interior, Apr–Oct; common in Fraser Valley, Nov–Mar.

Cooper's Hawk

Accipiter cooperii

Length: *Male:* 38–43 cm; *Female:* 43-48 cm
Wingspan: *Male:* 69–81 cm; *Female:* 81–94 cm

These speedy, aggressive raptors are an increasingly common sight in backyards, especially along the south coast, where they shoot in like kamikazes and snag a songbird caught unawares. Feathered balls of testosterone, Cooper's hawks will even take on squirrels or birds the size of rock pigeons. • This species is the most common of the "bird hawks" (*Accipiters*), distinguished by relatively short, rounded wings and long, rudder-like tails, which help aerial maneuverability in tight, wooded situations. **Where found:** mixed woodlands, riparian woodlands, urban gardens with feeders; common year-round along south coast; uncommon in southern ⅓ of province, Apr–Oct.

Red-tailed Hawk

Buteo jamaicensis

Length: *Male:* 46–58 cm; *Female:* 51–64 cm
Wingspan: 1.2–1.5 m

Common and widespread, red-tailed hawks are often seen along country roads, perched on fences or trees, and along freeways, perched on signs or trees where their white breasts render them conspicuous. They belong to a group of hawks known as Buteos, which typically soar in lazy circles or perch prominently, watching for prey. Red-tailed hawks have adapted well to urbanism and are commonly seen around cities. • The red-tailed hawk's piercing call is sometimes paired with the image of an eagle in TV commercials and movies. **Where found:** open to semi-open habitats; fairly common year-round on coast; uncommon in Interior, Apr–Oct.

American Kestrel

Falco sparverius

Length: 23–30 cm
Wingspan: 50–62 cm

The colourful American kestrel frequently perches on roadside wires or hovers over fields like an avian helicopter. This little falcon feeds on small rodents and in warmer months switches to a diet heavy in grasshoppers. • Most evidence suggests that kestrel populations are declining significantly in many areas, partially because of a lack of nesting holes. You could help these cavity-nesting falcons by erecting appropriate nest boxes in suitable habitat. **Where found:** open fields, grassy roadsides, agricultural landscapes; common throughout Interior, Apr–Oct; a few may overwinter in south.

Peregrine Falcon

Falco peregrinus

Length: *Male:* 38–43 cm; *Female:* 43–48 cm
Wingspan: 1.0–1.1 m

Nothing causes more panic in a flock of ducks or shore-birds than a hunting peregrine falcon. This agile raptor matches every twist and turn the flock makes, then dives to strike a lethal blow. • The peregrine falcon is the world's fastest bird. In a headfirst dive, it can reach speeds of up to 350 km/h. • Peregrine falcons represent a successful conservation effort since the banning of DDT in North America in 1972. In 1999, they were removed from the Endangered Species list. **Where found:** open marine, river and lakeshores, urban areas and open fields; nests on rocky cliffs or skyscraper ledges; uncommon resident on coast; rare, local in Okanagan Valley.

Sora

Porzana carolina

Length: 20–25 cm
Wingspan: 30–36 cm

Two loud plaintive whistles, followed by a loud, descending whinny announces the presence of the sora. Although you have probably never seen a sora, this reclusive bird can be surprisingly abundant in any type of marsh. • Rails have large, chicken-like feet for walking on aquatic vegetation, and they swim quite well over short distances. They can laterally compress their bodies to slip effortlessly through thick cattail stands. **Where found:** marshes, sloughs with abundant emergent vegetation; common in southern ½ of B.C. and northeast, May–Sept.

American Coot

Fulica americana

Length: 33–40 cm
Wingspan: 58–70 cm

Sometimes called "mudhens," coots are the extroverts of the rail world. While the rest of the clan remains hidden in wetland vegetation, coots swim in open water like ducks. Their individually webbed toes make them efficient swimmers and good divers, but they aren't above snatching a meal from another skilled diver. • In marshes where they breed, coots give loud, maniacal, "laughing" calls. Newly hatched young have distinct, reddish-orange down and bald, red crowns. **Where found:** shallow, open wetlands with emergent vegetation; locally common on south coast in winter; common in Interior, Apr–Oct.

Sandhill Crane

Grus canadensis

Length: 1.1–1.2 m
Wingspan: 1.8–2.1 m

Sandhill cranes have deep, rattling calls that resonate
from their coiled tracheas to carry great distances.
Migrating flocks sail on thermal updrafts, cir-
cling and gliding at such great heights that they
can scarcely be seen. In spring, cranes occasionally touch
down on open fields to perform spectacular courtship dances, calling, bowing and leaping with partially raised wings. In B.C., cranes have
traditional spots where they stage each year during migration. A few pairs still
breed in the Lower Mainland. **Where found:** agricultural fields and shorelines during
migration; local breeder in bogs; common migrant in Interior, uncommon on coast.

Killdeer

Charadrius vociferus

Length: 23–28 cm
Wingspan: 61 cm

When an intruder wanders too close to its nest, the
killdeer puts on its "broken wing" display. It greets
the interloper with piteous *kill-dee kill-dee* cries while dragging a wing and stum-
bling about as if injured. Most predators take the bait and follow, and once the
predator has been lured far away from the nest, the killdeer flies off with a loud
call. • This species has no doubt increased tremendously in modern times, as
human activities have increased suitable habitat. **Where found:** open fields, lakeshores, gravel streambeds, parking lots, large lawns; common throughout southern ½ of B.C., Apr–Nov; year-round on south coast.

Black Oystercatcher

Haematopus bachmani

Length: 43 cm
Wingspan: 79 cm

Black oystercatchers are devoted to their rocky shoreline habitat,
where their meals of limpets, mussels and snails are abundant.
Their flamboyant, red bills are well adapted for prying open tightly
sealed shells. • The young stay with their parents for up to a year
while they perfect their foraging technique and avoid predators such as
ravens and crows; if they survive the early perils of their first year, life at the beach can
be as long as 15 years! An estimated 30–35% of the world's population of black oystercatchers breed in B.C. **Where found:** rocky coastal shorelines and islands; breakwaters,
jetties and reefs; common year-round on outer coast, less common on inner coast.

Spotted Sandpiper

Actitis macularia

Length: 18–20 cm
Wingspan: 38 cm

In a rare case of sexual role-reversal, the female spotted sandpiper is the aggressor. She diligently defends her territory and may mate with several males, an unusual breeding strategy known as "polyandry." • Each summer, the female can lay up to 4 clutches and is capable of producing 20 eggs. She lays the eggs but does little else—the males tend the clutches. • Spotted sandpipers bob their tails constantly while on shore and fly with rapid, shallow, stiff-winged strokes, like a wire under tension that has been "twanged." **Where found:** shorelines, gravel beaches, swamps, sewage lagoons; common throughout, May–Sept.

Greater Yellowlegs

Tringa melanoleuca

Length: 33–38 cm
Wingspan: 68–70 cm

The greater yellowlegs and lesser yellowlegs (*T. flavipes*) are very similar medium-to-large sandpipers. Greaters have a much longer bill, thicker legs with noticeable "knees," and they utter a louder, more strident series of 3 or more whistles; lessers normally deliver 2. The overall body mass of a greater is nearly twice that of a lesser, something very apparent when the species are together. Yellowlegs are sometimes called "tell-tales": they alert all the shorebirds on a mudflat to invaders such as birders. **Where found:** shallow wetlands, shorelines, flooded fields; common migrant throughout; breeds locally in central B.C.

Black Turnstone

Arenaria melanocephala

Length: 23 cm
Wingspan: 80 cm

Black turnstones prefer rocky habitats, which they share with black oystercatchers, surfbirds (*Aphriza virgata*) and rock sandpipers (*Calidris ptilocnemis*). They are visual feeders that methodically search nooks and crannies in rocks and under seaweed for morsels. They hammer at barnacles and limpets to dislodge them and then extract the soft parts. • Feeding flocks are usually small, up to 100 birds, and even when eating they show a certain amount of aggression toward each other and other species. **Where found:** rocky coastal shorelines, breakwaters, jetties and reefs; may visit beaches with seaweed wracks as well as mudflats, gravel bars and temporary ponds; common along coast, Nov–Mar.

Western Sandpiper

Calidris mauri

Length: 15–18 cm
Wingspan: 36 cm

The western sandpiper is a member of a group of
sandpipers known as "peeps" in North America and
"stints" elsewhere in the English-speaking world. All
peeps are similar in plumage, but they are recognized as a group by their exuberant aerial maneuvers: flocks wheel over estuarine tidal flats. • The western sandpiper breeds only in Alaska and extreme northeastern Siberia but passes through our area in large numbers in migration and can be seen on most of our coast in winter. **Where found:** tidal estuaries, saltwater marshes, sandy beaches, freshwater shorelines, flooded fields and pools; abundant spring and autumn migrant along coast, less common inland.

Sanderling

Calidris alba

Length: 18–22 cm
Wingspan: 41–43 cm

Anyone who has spent time on a sandy coastal
beach between late summer and late spring has seen
sanderlings. Flocks of these charming shorebirds scamper
up and down the beach like mechanical toys, following every wave in pursuit of tiny crustaceans. If a wave catches a flock unprepared, the birds will rise in unison. Sanderlings also peck and probe with other sandpipers of sand and mudflats. **Where found:** primarily wide, clean sandy beaches, mudflats, estuaries, lakeshores; common to abundant on coast, Oct–Mar; uncommon migrant in south-central Interior.

Dunlin

Calidris alpina

Length: 19–23 cm
Wingspan: 43 cm

The dunlin is our most common winter shorebird and can often be seen in very large flocks,
flying or at tide-line roosts. Dynamic, swirling clouds of up
to 10,000 birds can be marvelled at as they fly wing
tip to wing tip in synchronised motion. • As spring
approaches, dunlins gradually take on their unmistakable breeding plumage of a reddish back and a bold black on the belly. **Where found:** tidal and saltwater marshes, estuaries, lagoon shorelines, open sandy ocean beaches, flooded fields and muddy wetlands; common to abundant on coast, Oct–Apr.

Long-billed Dowitcher

Limnodromus scolopaceus

Length: 28–32 cm
Wingspan: 48 cm

The beautiful breeding plumage of this shorebird makes it one of the most antici-pated returning migrants to our area. • Long-billed dowitchers favour freshwater habitats, even along the coast, preferring lakeshores, flooded pastures, grass-dotted marshes and the mouths of brackish tidal channels. They nest only along the Beaufort Sea in extreme northern Alaska and northwestern Canada. **Where found:** along lakeshores, shallow marshes and some areas of the coast; common autumn migrant on fresh water, especially in southern Peace R. region, Aug–Nov.

Wilson's Snipe

Gallinago delicata

Length: 27–29 cm
Wingspan: 46 cm

The winnowing of the Wilson's snipe is syn-onymous with spring evenings at a wetland. Snipes engage in spectacular aerial courtship displays, swooping and diving at great heights with their tails spread, produc-ing a "winnowing" sound that is made by air rushing past the outer tail feathers. The sound has been described as comparable to a boreal owl's call. • Well-camouflaged snipes are often concealed by vegetation. When flushed from cover, the snipe utters a harsh *skape* note and then flies in a low, rapid zigzag pattern to confuse would-be predators. **Where found:** freshwater and saltwater habitats, including marshes, meadows, wetlands; found locally year-round on coast; common in Interior, Apr–Oct.

Wilson's Phalarope

Phalaropus tricolor

Length: 21–24 cm
Wingspan: 36–40 cm

Phalaropes are the wind-up toys of the bird world: they spin and whirl about in tight circles, stirring up the water. Then, with needle-like bills, they pick out the aquatic insects and small crustaceans that funnel toward the surface. • With all phala-ropes, sexual roles are reversed; the larger, more colourful female may mate with several males. The female lays the eggs, but the male incubates them and tends the young. **Where found:** marshes, wet meadows, sewage lagoons, lakeshores during migration; uncommon to common in southern Interior, Apr–Oct.

Bonaparte's Gull

Chroicocephalus philadelphia

Length: 30–36 cm
Wingspan: 84 cm

Small and buoyant on the wing, Bonaparte's gulls are very different from their larger, cruder brethren. This species doesn't scavenge fries in McDonald's parking lots—largely piscivorous, they snare small fish adeptly from the water's surface. Spring migrants and breeding birds are resplendent with black heads, as if the birds were dunked in dark paint. By late fall, the black is gone, but the birds still display conspicuous, white, primary wedges on the wings and fly with a tern-like grace lacking in larger gulls. **Where found:** breeds in coniferous forests near water; abundant coastal estuaries and sewage lagoons, Mar–Apr, Sept–Nov; common in Interior lakes, wetlands, rivers, Apr–Oct.

Ring-billed Gull

Larus delawarensis

Length: 46–51 cm
Wingspan: 1.2 m

Few people can claim to never having seen this common, widespread gull. Highly tolerant of humans, the ring-billed gull eats almost anything and swarms parks, beaches, golf courses and fast-food restaurant parking lots looking for food handouts. It is a 3-year gull, first acquiring adult plumage in its third calendar year of life, after going through a series of sub-adult moults. In B.C., ring-bills nest on Okanagan Lake, Shuswap Lake, Quesnel River and Fraser Lake. **Where found:** small, barren islands during breeding; lakes, rivers, landfills, parking lots, fields, parks in migration; common in southern B.C., Apr–Oct.

Glaucous-winged Gull

Larus glaucescens

Length: 60–67 cm
Wingspan: 1.3 m

Big, bold and largely married to salt water, the pale-backed glaucous-winged gull is the most common gull found along the B.C. coast. • Adult birds have indistinct white "mirrors" at the ends of their grey wing tips. Scattered immature remain along the coast as their drab, brownish, first-winter plumage changes into that of the handsome adult at 4 years of age. **Where found:** saltwater and brackish bays, estuaries, harbours and open ocean; also buildings and bridges; common to locally abundant year-round on coast.

Common Tern

Sterna hirundo

Length: 33–40 cm
Wingspan: 76 cm

Sleek common terns patrol the shorelines of lakes, rivers and sea coasts in B.C. during spring and autumn migration, characteristically hovering over the water, looking for small fishes near the surface. They capture their prey with spectacular aerial dives. • Terns are effortless fliers and impressive long-distance migrants. One common tern banded in Great Britain was recovered in Australia, setting a new world record for long-distance migration. **Where found:** large lakes, slow-moving rivers, wetlands; common migrant on inner coast, esp. in autumn; uncommon migrant in south-central Interior; rare elsewhere.

Common Murre

Uria aalge

Length: 41–44 cm
Wingspan: 66 cm

Common murres spend much of their lives at sea and only come ashore to breed, nesting in huge, tightly packed colonies of up to tens of thousands of birds. • Pelagic boat tours are a fantastic way to see common murres in action. These skilled swimmers use their small wings, webbed feet and sleek, waterproof plumage to pursue fish underwater. Murres can remain beneath the surface for more than a minute and regularly dive to depths of 40 m. **Where found:** Breeding: offshore islands, islets and rocks. Foraging: open ocean from just beyond the surf zone to miles offshore; found locally year round, most common on outer coast.

Pigeon Guillemot

Cepphus columba

Length: 30–35 cm
Wingspan: 59 cm

Pigeon guillemots are among the most widespread and commonly seen alcids along the Pacific coast. Their bright red feet and scarlet mouth lining are unmistakable. Courting birds flirt outrageously, waving their flamboyant feet, peering down each other's throats and emitting wheezy whistles. • During the summer months, these seabirds forage just offshore. They dive underwater to feed, paddling quickly with their small wings and steering with their feet. **Where found:** breeds on rocky offshore islands; also docks, wharves or piers; common year-round on south coast and Apr–Oct on north coast.

Marbled Murrelet

Brachyramphus marmoratus

Length: 23–35 cm
Wingspan: 41cm

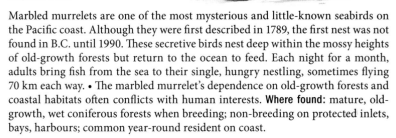

Marbled murrelets are one of the most mysterious and little-known seabirds on the Pacific coast. Although they were first described in 1789, the first nest was not found in B.C. until 1990. These secretive birds nest deep within the mossy heights of old-growth forests but return to the ocean to feed. Each night for a month, adults bring fish from the sea to their single, hungry nestling, sometimes flying 70 km each way. • The marbled murrelet's dependence on old-growth forests and coastal habitats often conflicts with human interests. **Where found:** mature, old-growth, wet coniferous forests when breeding; non-breeding on protected inlets, bays, harbours; common year-round resident on coast.

Tufted Puffin

Fratercula cirrhata

Length: 38 cm
Wingspan: 64 cm

Famous for their flamboyant bills and cavalier head tufts, tufted puffins are an added attraction on West Coast whale-watching tours. • A puffin can line up more than 12 small fish crosswise in its bill, using its round tongue and serrated upper mandible to keep the hoard in place. • Stubby wings propel alcids with surprising speed and agility underwater, but these features make for awkward takeoffs and laborious flight. **Where found:** *Breeding:* offshore islands with soil burrows; upwellings near islands. *Winter:* deep, offshore ocean.

Rock Pigeon

Columba livia

Length: 31–33 cm
Wingspan: 71 cm

Formerly called rock doves, these Old World pigeons are one of the world's most recognized birds. They have been domesticated for about 6500 years; because of their ability to return to far-flung locales, they are often bred as "homing pigeons." In the wild, rock pigeons breed on cliffs; their urban counterparts nest on building ledges or under bridges. • All pigeons and doves feed to their young a nutritious liquid produced in their crop called "pigeon milk" (it's not real milk). **Where found:** urban areas, railyards, agricultural areas; common year-round in southern ½ of B.C. and in southern Peace R. region.

Great Horned Owl

Bubo virginianus

Length: 46–64 cm
Wingspan: 90–150 cm

Great horned owls occur in all manner of habitats. This powerful predator can take mammals the size of small house cats. Even skunks are not safe; this bird is one of few predators not put off by the malodorous discharges of the striped beasts. • Great horned owls begin their courtship as early as January, and by February and March, the females are incubating eggs. These owls often nest on crow or hawk stick nests and may be spotted by their "ears" projecting above the nest. **Where found:** everywhere from open agricultural landscapes to marshes with scattered woodlots, urban areas; uncommon year-round resident throughout.

Barred Owl

Strix varia

Length: 43–61 cm
Wingspan: 1.0–1.3 m

The maniacal cacophony produced by calling barred owls is unforgettable; the caterwauling is enough to scare the uninitiated out of the woods. Their typical call is a series of hoots that sounds like *Who cooks for you? Who cooks for you all?* • Most barred owls occur in swampy woods or densely forested ravines; they do best near water. Increasing numbers are turning up in heavily treed suburbia, a sign of their adaptability. **Where found:** mature coniferous and mixed forests, especially near water; uncommon year-round resident in southern ⅔ of province.

Northern Saw-whet Owl

Aegolius acadicus

Length: 18–23 cm
Wingspan: 43–55 cm

Although primarily predators of forest mice, northern saw-whet owls are opportunistic hunters that take whatever they can, whenever they can. By day, saw-whets roost quietly in the cover of dense lower branches and brush to avoid attracting mobbing forest songbirds. A race of saw-whet owl living on Haida Gwaii (Queen Charlotte Is.) is unique not only in structure but in the food it eats. Unlike other owls, much of its diet consists of marine invertebrates captured at low tide. **Where found:** coniferous and mixed forests; wooded city parks and ravines; uncommon to locally common in southern ½ of B.C.

Common Nighthawk

Chordeiles minor

Length: 22–25 cm
Wingspan: 61 cm

Displaying nighthawks put on
dramatic aerial courtship displays. The male flutters high over nesting sites, uttering nasal *peent* notes, and then dives with his wings extended. At the bottom of the dive, wind rushing through the primary feathers produces a hollow, booming sound. • The nighthawk also feeds in midair. Feather shafts that surround its large, gaping mouth funnel insects into its bill. • Resting nighthawks sit lengthwise on tree branches and can be nearly invisible. **Where found:** open and semi-open country, nests on rooftops in suburban, urban areas; absent from north coast; uncommon to locally abundant elsewhere, May–Sept.

Vaux's Swift

Chaetura vauxi

Length: 13 cm
Wingspan: 31 cm

Resembling flying cigars, swifts are more at home on the
wing than perched. Indeed, they cannot perch like most birds;
they must prop themselves against a vertical surface using their stiff tails for support. Feeding, drinking, bathing, even nest material collection and mating is all accomplished while they fly! The Vaux's swift is the smallest swift in North America and arrives in B.C. in late April or early May. **Where found:** *Breeding:* mixed woods and forest with cavities, rivers, urban areas. *In migration:* open sky over forests or lakes, rivers; common in southern ⅔ of B.C., Apr–Oct.

Anna's Hummingbird

Calypte anna

Length: 8–10 cm
Wingspan: 12–14 cm

Once restricted as a nesting species to the
Pacific slope of northern Baja California and south-
ern California, Anna's hummingbird expanded its range northward along the coast after the 1930s, and today, we get to enjoy this beautiful hummer. • Hummingbirds are easily lured to our gardens with exotic, nectar-producing plants and/or hummingbird feeders. **Where found:** riparian areas, coastal scrubland, farmlands and urban gardens; common year-round resident of southeastern Vancouver Is.; uncommon on south mainland coast; rare in Okanagan Valley.

99

Rufous Hummingbird

Selasphorus rufus

Length: 8–9 cm
Wingspan: 11 cm

Rufous hummingbirds are tiny, delicate avian jewels, but their beauty hides a relentless mean streak—these birds buzz past one another at nectar sites and chase rivals for some distances. • Hummingbirds beat their wings up to 80 times per second, their hearts can beat up to 1200 times per minute, and they are capable of flying at speeds up to 100 km/h. **Where found:** nearly any habitat with abundant flowers, including gardens; edges of coniferous and deciduous forests; burned sites; brushy slopes and alpine meadows; common throughout, except northeast B.C.

Belted Kingfisher

Megaceryle alcyon

Length: 28–36 cm
Wingspan: 51 cm

Chronically antisocial other than during the brief nesting period, kingfishers stake out productive fishing grounds and scold invaders with loud rattling calls. They catch fish with headfirst plunges, and often beat the victim into submission by rapping it against a branch. • Mating pairs nest in a chamber at the end of a long tunnel dug into an earth bank. • With a red band across her belly, the female kingfisher is more colourful than her mate. **Where found:** lakes, ponds, rivers; fairly common throughout, Apr–Oct; year-round on south coast.

Downy Woodpecker

Picoides pubescens

Length: 15–18 cm
Wingspan: 30 cm

Easily our most common woodpecker, the downy is found everywhere from backyard feeders to dense forest. It closely resembles the less common hairy woodpecker (*P. villosus*, found throughout B.C.) but is much smaller, with a proportionately tiny bill and black spots on the white outer tail feathers. • Downies and other woodpeckers have feathered nostrils that filter out sawdust produced by their excavations, and long barbed tongues that can reach far into crevices to extract grubs and other morsels. **Where found:** deciduous and mixed forests, residential yards; common year-round in southern ⅔ of province.

Northern Flicker

Colaptes auratus

"red-shafted" flicker

Length: 32–33 cm
Wingspan: 51 cm

The northern flicker spends much of its time on the ground, feeding on ants. Flickers also clean themselves by squashing ants and preening themselves with the remains. Ants contain formic acid, which kills small parasites on the birds' skin and feathers. • When these woodpeckers fly, they reveal a bold white rump and colourful underwings. The "red-shafted" race has salmon-coloured underwings and is common and widespread in B.C., especially in southern and coastal areas. The "yellow-shafted" race, found in northeastern B.C., has yellow underwings. **Where found:** open woodlands, forest edges, fields, wetlands, treed suburbia; common year-round in southern ½ of B.C. and from Apr–Oct elsewhere.

Olive-sided Flycatcher

Contopus cooperi

Length: 19 cm
Wingspan: 33 cm

The olive-sided flycatcher introduces the largest order of birds in B.C.—the Passeriformes—also referred to as passerines, songbirds or perching birds. The olive-sided flycatcher's upright, attentive posture contrasts with its comical song: *quick-three-beers! quick-three-beers!* During nesting, this flycatcher changes its tune to an equally enthusiastic *pip-pip-pip*. Its twig nest is bound with spider silk and built high in a conifer, usually on a branch far from the trunk. • This bird's numbers are declining, and it is threatened on the coast. **Where found:** semi-open mixed and coniferous forests near water; prefers burned areas and wetlands; uncommon throughout, Apr–Oct.

Pacific-slope Flycatcher

Empidonax difficilis

Length: 13 cm
Wingspan: 20 cm

Flycatchers are hard to distinguish from each other, and it was not until late in the 20th century that the Pacific-slope flycatcher was recognized as its own species. Nevertheless, it is a common songbird in our area, and its song is more distinctive than its looks. The upslurred *suweeet* call is a familiar sound in any moist woodland in spring. • This flycatcher sits perched on exposed branches, stalking its insect prey that it swoops down on to catch, or "hawk," in flight. **Where found:** moist hardwood or mixed forests in foothills and valleys; common on coast, uncommon in central and southern Interior, Apr–Oct.

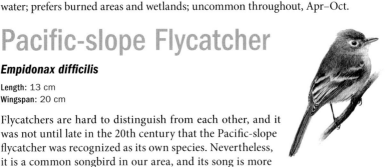

Western Kingbird

Tyrannus verticalis

Length: 20–23 cm
Wingspan: 38–41 cm

Kingbirds are a group of flycatchers that perch on wires or fence posts in open habitats and fearlessly chase out larger birds from their breeding territories. • In tumbling aerial courtship displays, the male flies to heights of 20 m above the ground, stalls, then tumbles and flips his way back to earth. • The eastern kingbird *(T. tyrannus)* occurs in central and south Interior of B.C. **Where found:** *Breeding:* open country near farm buildings, woodlands or orchards; any fairly open habitat during migration; common in Okanagan Valley, uncommon northward, May–Aug.

Northern Shrike

Lanius excubitor

Length: 25 cm
Wingspan: 37 cm

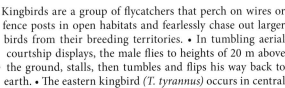

Shrikes are predatory birds that kill and eat small birds or rodents, swooping down on them from above. Northern shrikes lack powerful talons and rely on their sharp, hooked bills to catch prey. Males display their hunting competence to females by impaling their prey on thorns or barbed wire (this may also be a means of storing excess food). **Where found:** open country, including fields, forest clearings, shrubby riparian areas, shrubby roadsides; uncommon in southern ½ of B.C., Oct–Mar; breeds in extreme northwest B.C.

Warbling Vireo

Vireo gilvus

Length: 13 cm
Wingspan: 21 cm

The charming warbling vireo is a common spring and summer resident, often settling close to urban areas; its velvety voice has a warbling quality not heard in other vireos and is more distinctive than its looks—it lacks any splashy field marks. • The warbling vireo nests in a horizontal fork of a tree or shrub, making a hanging basket-like cup nest of grass, roots, plant down and spider silk. **Where found:** *Breeding:* mainly open, mixed forests with shrubby understorey. *In migration:* almost any woodlands; prefers hardwood stands and shrublands; common throughout, Apr–Oct; absent from north coast.

Gray Jay

Perisoreus canadensis

Length: 29 cm
Wingspan: 46 cm

Few birds exceed mischievous gray jays for curiosity and
boldness. Attracted by any foreign sound or potential
feeding opportunity, small family groups glide gently
and unexpectedly out of spruce stands to introduce
themselves to any passersby. These intelligent birds are known to hide bits of food
under the bark of trees, to be retrieved in times of need. • Gray jays nest earlier
than other songbirds in our region, laying their eggs in late February. The young
regularly fledge before the snow melts. **Where found:** coniferous forests; uncommon to locally common throughout, year-round. **Also known as:** Canada jay,
whiskey jack, camp robber.

Steller's Jay

Cyanocitta stelleri

Length: 29 cm
Wingspan: 48 cm

With a dark crest and velvet blue feathers, the stunning
Steller's jay is a resident jewel in B.C. and was named the
provincial bird in 1987. Generally noisy and pugnacious,
this bird suddenly becomes silent and cleverly elusive
when nesting. • Over the past 2 decades, the eastern
blue jay *(C. cristata)* has been expanding its range
into the Steller jay's territory with some oddball
hybrids appearing. **Where found:** coniferous and mixed woodlands; uncommon
year-round in southern ½ of B.C.

Black-billed Magpie

Pica hudsonia

Length: 46 cm
Wingspan: 64 cm

Truly among North America's
most beautiful birds, the black-billed magpie is also very
intelligent and resourceful. In its constant search for food,
the bird will pluck ticks off the backs of large mammals and
turn over stones for grubs. • These exceptional architects
construct large, domed stick nests that conceal and protect eggs and young from
harsh weather and predators. Abandoned nests remain in trees for years and are
often re-used by other birds. **Where found:** farmyards, hedgerows, open groves, suburbia; common year-round from Prince George south; also extreme northwest
corner; absent from coast.

103

American Crow

Corvus brachyrhynchos

Length: 43–53 cm
Wingspan: 94 cm

One of our most intelligent birds, the crow has in recent years occupied urban places in much greater numbers. It knows it is safe from hunters—the crow is legal game in many areas—and towns offer this opportunistic scavenger abundant food. • Crows will drop clams from great heights onto a hard surface to crack the shells, one of the few examples of birds using objects to manipulate food. • Very social, crows sometimes form massive winter roosts that can number into the thousands. **Where found:** nearly ubiquitous; urban areas, agricultural fields, forests; year-round from Prince George south; absent from coast where it is replaced by the northwestern crow (*C. caurinus*).

Common Raven

Corvus corax

Length: 61 cm
Wingspan: 1.3 m

Glorified in Native cultures throughout the Northern Hemisphere, the raven has earned a reputation as a crafty, clever bird. This adaptable, widespread bird uses its wits to survive along coastlines, in deserts, in temperate regions, on arctic tundra and in suburbia. The raven produces complex vocalizations, forms lifelong pair bonds and exhibits problem-solving skills. When working as a pair to confiscate a meal, one raven may act as the decoy while the other steals the food. **Where found:** nearly ubiquitous; urban areas, forests, landfills; year-round throughout.

Horned Lark

Eremophila alpestris

Length: 18 cm
Wingspan: 30 cm

Seemingly nondescript, horned larks scurry like mice across the most barren landscapes. They often flush from rural roadsides as cars pass by; watch for the blackish tail that contrasts with the sandy-coloured body. A good look at perched larks reveals a black mask, twin tiny horns and pale yellow underparts smudged with a dark crescent across the chest. Listen for their clear, tinkling calls in open agricultural lands. **Where found:** open areas, pastures, prairies, cultivated fields; common migrant and uncommon in summer throughout Interior B.C.; rare on coast and in northeast.

Violet-green Swallow

Tachycineta thalassina

Length: 13 cm
Wingspan: 36 cm

Their affinity for cliffs, open areas, natural tree cavities and nest boxes allows violet-green swallows to inhabit diverse habitats. • Swallows are swift and graceful fliers, routinely travelling at speeds of 40 km/h. They catch flying insects such as flies, flying ants and wasps, often foraging far higher than other swallows, and drink on the wing by skimming the water's surface. **Where found:** wide variety of open areas near water, including open woodlands, wooded canyons, agricultural lands and towns; common throughout southern ½ of B.C., uncommon northward, Apr–Oct; absent from northeast.

Barn Swallow

Hirundo rustica

Length: 18 cm
Wingspan: 32–34 cm

Barn swallows are familiar sights under bridges and picnic shelters or around farmsteads, where they nest in barns and other buildings. It is now almost unheard of for them to nest in natural sites such as cliffs, to which they once were restricted. Their nests are constructed by rolling mud into small balls, one mouthful of mud at a time. • In males, the long forked tail is a sign of vigour; longer-tailed males tend to live longer and have higher reproductive success. **Where found:** forages in open country, nests on human-made structures and cliffs; common throughout, May–Sept.

Black-capped Chickadee

Poecile atricapillus

Length: 13–15 cm
Wingspan: 20 cm

Curious and inquisitive, black-capped chickadees have been known to land on people. They are very common and familiar visitors to backyard feeders. Chickadees cache seeds and are able to relocate hidden food up to a month later. • Chickadees are omnivorous cavity nesters that usually lay 6 to 8 eggs in late winter or early spring. • On cold winter nights, chickadees may huddle together in the shelter of tree cavities or other suitable hollows. **Where found:** mixed and deciduous forests, parks, suburban backyards; absent from coast; common elsewhere, year-round.

Chestnut-backed Chickadee

Poecile rufescens

Length: 12 cm
Wingspan: 18 cm

A chestnut-backed chickadee could fit in the palm of your hand, but these energetic little birds would hardly sit still long enough. They prefer to flit through the forest and scour for insects or descend on bird feeders in merry mobs. To view these friendly birds up close, mount a platform feeder on your window ledge. • On chilly winter days, chickadees must work hard to survive. They sometimes depend on food stores stashed during the summer, and they stay warm by snuggling together in crevices or woodpecker cavities. **Where found:** forests of any kind, urban and residential areas; common year-round on coast and far southern B.C., rare elsewhere.

Bushtit

Psaltriparus minimus

Length: 11 cm
Wingspan: 15 cm

Bushtits catch your eye as they endlessly bounce from one shrubby perch to another and catch your ear with charming, bell-like, tinkling calls. Hyperactive in everything they do, these tiny, fluffy, gregarious birds are constantly on the move, either fastidiously building a nest or roaming about in post-breeding bands of up to 40 members. When nest building, they neurotically test every fibre to ensure its suitability. Bushtits will desert both nest and mate if intruded upon. **Where found:** shrubby forests, urban and residential settings; common year-round on southeastern Vancouver Is., Gulf Is., Sunshine Coast and Fraser R. valley to Hope.

Red-breasted Nuthatch

Sitta canadensis

Length: 11 cm
Wingspan: 22 cm

The red-breasted nuthatch has a somewhat dizzying view of the world as it moves down tree trunks headfirst, searching for bark-dwelling insects. Red-breasted nuthatches stage periodic southward invasions some winters, which are termed irruptions. Thus, they may be absent at feeders some winters and common the next. Irruptions are triggered by food shortages, not weather. Nuthatches are especially attracted to backyard feeders filled with suet or peanut butter. **Where found:** coniferous and mixed forests; common year-round in southern ½ of B.C.

Winter Wren

Troglodytes troglodytes

Length: 10 cm
Wingspan: 13 cm

The upraised, mottled brown tail of the winter wren
blends well with its habitat of gnarled, upturned roots and
decomposing tree trunks. • This tiny bird has a great vocal
magnitude—it boldly lays claim to its territory with its call
and distinctive, melodious song. The winter wren can sustain
its song for 10 seconds, using up to 113 tones. • Although the male winter wren
contributes to raising the family by defending the nest and finding food for the
nestlings, he sleeps elsewhere at night, in an unfinished nest. **Where found:** lowland
forests, woodlands and thickets, preferring wet forests; common year-round on
coast; common throughout southern ½ of B.C., May–Oct.

American Dipper

Cinclus mexicanus

Length: 19 cm
Wingspan: 28 cm

When you come across a small, dark bird
standing on an exposed boulder next to a fast-
flowing mountain stream, you have no doubt
found an American dipper. This unique, aquatic songbird
bends its legs incessantly, bobbing to the roar of the torrent, then suddenly
dives into the water. It uses its wings to swim in search of aquatic insect larvae.
Where found: fast-flowing, rocky streams and rivers with cascades, riffles and waterfalls; locally uncommon year-round throughout but absent from northwest B.C.

Golden-crowned Kinglet

Regulus satrapa

Length: 10 cm
Wingspan: 18 cm

Our smallest songbird, golden-crowned
kinglets are impossibly tiny, barely larger
than ruby-throated hummingbirds. They are
rather tame and can often be coaxed closer by making squeaking or "pishing" sounds. Identify kinglets
from afar by their perpetual motion and chronic, ner-
vous wing flicking. Like chickadees, kinglets can lower their body temperature at
night to conserve energy. **Where found:** nests in conifers; in deciduous and mixed
forest and woodlands in winter; uncommon in summer and common in winter
on coast; common in summer and uncommon in winter in Interior.

Mountain Bluebird

Sialia currucoides

Length: 18 cm
Wingspan: 36 cm

The vibrant mountain bluebird looks like a piece of sky come to life. It perches on wire fences and tall grasses, alighting to snatch up insects on the ground or hovering briefly to pluck at berries. • Natural nest sites, such as woodpecker cavities or holes in sandstone cliffs, are in high demand. Habitat loss and increased competition with aggressive European starlings for these sites have forced many mild-mannered bluebirds to nest in artificial nest boxes. **Where found:** open forests, forest edges, burned forests, agricultural areas and grasslands; uncommon on coast; common throughout Interior, becoming uncommon northward, Apr–Oct.

Swainson's Thrush

Catharus ustulatus

Length: 18 cm
Wingspan: 30 cm

Swainson's thrush shares the speckled breast of other thrushes, as well as the habit of foraging on the ground for insects and other invertebrates. But unlike its relatives, it may hover-glean from the airy heights of trees like a warbler or vireo. • The Swainson's thrush is a wary bird and often gives its sharp warning call from a distance, offering little chance to be seen. Perched atop the tallest tree in its territory, the male Swainson's is one of the last forest songsters to be silenced by nightfall. **Where found:** forest and thickets; common throughout, Apr–Oct.

American Robin

Turdus migratorius

Length: 25 cm
Wingspan: 43 cm

Flocks of American robins arrive in March to welcome spring with their cheery songs. Among our most widely seen, familiar and easily recognized birds, robins occur nearly everywhere. Striking males have black heads, rich brick-red underparts and streaked white throats. • Robins are master earthworm-hunters, adeptly spotting a worm and tugging it from the soil. In winter, they switch to a diet of berries. **Where found:** habitat generalist, residential lawns, gardens, urban parks, forests, bogs; common throughout, Mar–Nov but may overwinter near fruit-bearing trees and springs.

European Starling

Sturnus vulgaris

Length: 22 cm
Wingspan: 41 cm

We can thank the Shakespeare Society for this species, which is perhaps the most damaging non-native bird introduced in North America. About 60 European starlings were released in New York City in 1890 and 1891 as part of an ill-fated effort to release into the U.S. all the birds mentioned in Shakespeare's works. Now abundant throughout North America, long-lived starlings often drive native species such as bluebirds from nest cavities. **Where found:** cities, towns, farmyards, woodland fringes, clearings; abundant year-round in south; common in northeastern B.C., Apr–Oct.

Cedar Waxwing

Bombycilla cedrorum

Length: 18 cm
Wingspan: 30 cm

Graceful and dapper, cedar waxwings have a decidedly suave look. Although largely frugivorous (fruit eating), waxwings engage in lots of flycatching in summer along the riparian areas where they often nest. • Cedar waxwings inhabit the southern half of B.C. in summer but migrate south of the border for winter. Slightly larger bohemian waxwings *(B. garrulus)* breed in northern B.C., then form nomadic winter flocks and wander about the southern Interior, plundering berries from fruiting trees. **Where found:** wooded residential parks and gardens, overgrown fields, riparian areas; common and nomadic summer visitor to southern mainland; uncommon on offshore islands.

Yellow Warbler

Dendroica petechia

Length: 13 cm
Wingspan: 20 cm

Warblers are among our most beautiful birds, and the yellow warbler is one of our showiest. It sings a loud, ringing *sweet-sweet-I'm-so-sweet* song. • This warbler is often parasitized by the brown-headed cowbird and has learned to recognize cowbird eggs. But instead of tossing the foreign eggs out, the yellow warbler will build another nest overtop the old eggs or abandon the nest completely. Occasionally, cowbirds strike repeatedly—a 5-storey nest was once found! **Where found:** habitat generalist; moist, open woodlands, scrubby meadows, urban parks and gardens; common throughout, May–Aug.

109

Yellow-rumped Warbler

"Myrtle" Warbler

"Audubon's" Warbler

Dendroica coronata

Length: 13–15 cm
Wingspan: 23 cm

Yellow-rumped warblers are the most abundant and widespread wood-warblers in North America. There are 2 races of the yellow-rumped warbler, the "Myrtle warbler," which has a white throat, and the "Audubon's warbler," which has a yellow throat. In general, "Audubon's warblers" are more abundant in the south, and "Myrtle warblers" are more abundant north of Prince George. **Where found:** mature coniferous and mixed woodlands; *Coast:* common migrant, less common in summer, may overwinter. *Interior:* common throughout, Apr–Oct.

Common Yellowthroat

Geothlypis trichas

Length: 11–14 cm
Wingspan: 18 cm

The little masked bandit's loud *witchity witchity witchity* song bursting from the cattails gives away this skulker. The common yellowthroat is probably our most common breeding warbler, reaching peak numbers in wetlands and damp overgrown fields. It has wren-like curiosity, and you can coax it into view by making squeaking or "pishing" sounds. The female can be confusing to identify but shares the male's odd big-headed, slender-bodied, long-legged dimensions. **Where found:** wetlands, riparian areas, wet, overgrown meadows; common throughout, May–Sept.

Wilson's Warbler

Wilsonia pusilla

Length: 10 cm
Wingspan: 18 cm

The petite Wilson's warbler darts energetically through the undergrowth in its tireless search for insects. Fueled by its energy-rich prey, this indefatigable bird seems to behave as if a motionless moment would break some unwritten law of warblerdom. • This bird is named for ornithologist Alexander Wilson, who pioneered studies of North American birds. **Where found:** wet thickets and shrubby mixedwood habitats, riparian area; common throughout, Apr–Oct.

Western Tanager

Piranga ludoviciana

Length: 18 cm
Wingspan: 29 cm

The western tanager brings with it the colours
of a tropical visitor on its summer vacation in our
area. This bird raises a new generation of young
and takes advantage of the seasonal explosion of food in our
forests before heading back to its exotic wintering grounds in Mexico and Central
America. • The male western tanager spends long periods of time singing from the
same perch, sounding like a robin with a sore throat. **Where found:** almost any forested
habitat, including gardens; prefers mature coniferous and mixed forests for breeding;
common on southeastern Vancouver Is. and throughout Interior, Apr–Oct.

Spotted Towhee

Pipilo maculatus

Length: 18–21 cm
Wingspan: 26 cm

Towhees are large, colourful, chunky sparrows with long
tails. • These noisy birds are often heard before they are seen
as they rustle about in dense undergrowth. They employ an
unusual 2-footed shuffling technique to uncover food items. • The
spotted towhee sings several hurried notes followed by a buzzy trill:
che che che che che zheee! **Where found:** brushy hedgerows and woods
with a dense understorey; overgrown bushy fields and hillsides; frequently at
feeders; common year-round on south coast and from Apr–Oct in south Interior.

Chipping Sparrow

Spizella passerina

Length: 13–15 cm
Wingspan: 22 cm

The chipping sparrow can be distinguished from other
sparrows by its rufous crown and prominent white
"eyebrow." This bird's trilling song, however, is very
similar to that of the dark-eyed junco. Listen for the
chipping sparrow's rapid trill, which is slightly
faster, drier and less musical. • Commonly nesting at eye level or lower,
some chipping sparrow nests are so poorly constructed that eggs can be seen
through the nest materials. **Where found:** open coniferous or mixed woodland edges,
shrubby yards, gardens; absent from north coast, common elsewhere May–Sept.

Song Sparrow

Melospiza melodia

Length: 15–17 cm
Wingspan: 20 cm

Widespread, adaptable and ubiquitous song sparrows are likely in your backyard. They have one of the most beautiful songs of any bird: a bright, variable series of clear notes and trills. Song sparrows have a bold, central breast spot and a long, rounded tail, which is conspicuous as the bird is flying away. • Margaret Morse Nice of Columbus, Ohio, studied this species extensively and published groundbreaking research on song sparrows in the 1930s and '40s, a time when the role of women in biology was largely non-existent. **Where found:** shrublands, riparian thickets, suburban gardens, fields; common year-round on coast and southern B.C. and from Apr–Oct elsewhere.

White-crowned Sparrow

Zonotrichia leucophrys

Length: 17–18 cm
Wingspan: 23 cm

Large, bold and smartly patterned white-crowned sparrows brighten brushy hedgerows, overgrown fields and riparian areas. • Several different races of the white-crowned sparrow occur in North America, all with similar plumage but different song dialects. Research into this sparrow has given science tremendous insight into bird physiology, homing behaviour and the geographic variability of song dialects. **Where found:** shrubby, mature aspen or mixedwood forests; may visit residential areas; common in central and northern areas, Apr–Oct; uncommon winter visitor on inner south coast.

Dark-eyed Junco

"Oregon" Junco

Junco hyemalis

Length: 14–17 cm
Wingspan: 23 cm

"Slate-coloured" Junco

Juncos are one of North America's most abundant songbirds, with a total population estimated at 630 million birds. When flushed, dark-eyed juncos flash prominent, white outer tail feathers. These feathers may serve as "lures" for raptors; a pursuing hawk fixates on the white flashes and will grab only a few tail feathers, enabling the junco to escape. • There are 5 closely related dark-eyed junco subspecies in North America that share similar habits but differ in colouration and range. The rufous-sided, black-hooded "Oregon junco" and the mostly grey "slate-coloured junco" regularly occur in B.C. **Where found:** shrubby woodland borders and backyard feeders; common year-round throughout; overwinter in south.

112

Red-winged Blackbird

Agelaius phoeniceus

Length: 18–24 cm
Wingspan: 33 cm

Red-winged blackbirds are one of North America's most abundant birds. Males are stunning, and when they court females by thrusting their wings forward to flare the brilliant scarlet-orange epaulets, they appear as grand as any of our birds. • Males are avian polygamists that may have 15 females in their territory. • True harbingers of spring, they make loud, raspy *konk-a-ree* calls that can be heard in early April. **Where found:** cattail marshes, wet meadows, ditches, agricultural areas, overgrown fields; rare on north coast, common to abundant elsewhere, Apr–Oct ; may overwinter in south.

Western Meadowlark

Sturnella neglecta

Length: 24 cm
Wingspan: 40 cm

This bird's clear, ringing, whistled songs are characteristic sounds of grasslands and fields. • From above, meadowlarks are muted in sombre hues of speckled brown, allowing them to blend with the vegetation. Seen from below, their striking, lemon-yellow breast is struck across with a bold, black chevron. When flushed, meadowlarks reveal conspicuous, white outer tail feathers, and they fly with distinctive stiff, shallow wingbeats. **Where found:** grassy meadows, roadsides, pastures, agricultural areas; uncommon and local on southern Vancouver Is. in winter; common in southern Interior, Apr–Oct.

Brown-headed Cowbird

Molothrus ater

Length: 15–20 cm
Wingspan: 30 cm

Cowbirds are reviled as nest parasites: they lay their eggs in other birds' nests and are known to parasitize more than 140 bird species. Upon hatching, baby cowbirds out-compete the host's young, leading to nest failure. This strange habit evolved with the birds' association with nomadic bison herds. As the animals moved about, cowbirds were not in one place long enough to tend their own nests. Cowbirds haven't forgotten their roots and still commonly forage around cattle. **Where found:** agricultural and residential areas, woodland edges, now nearly ubiquitous; common throughout from May–Aug, except northern coast and northeastern B.C.; may overwinter in extreme southwest.

Purple Finch

Carpodacus purpureus

Length: 13–15 cm
Wingspan: 25 cm

Male purple finches are more raspberry red than purple. The male finch often delivers his musical warble from an exposed perch at the top of a live tree. • Purple finches are particularly attracted to sunflower seeds, and small flocks can be lured to southern feeders in winter. However, they are cyclically irruptive; during some winters many more move south than in other years. **Where found:** coniferous and mixed forests; common year-round on south coast and from Apr–Oct in northern B.C.

House Finch

Carpodacus mexicanus

Length: 12–15 cm
Wingspan: 22–25 cm

Formerly restricted to the arid Southwest U.S. and Mexico, the house finch is now commonly found throughout the continental U.S. and southern Canada. In B.C., a nesting pair was first discovered at Penticton in 1935. Only the resourceful house finch has been aggressive and stubborn enough to successfully out-compete the house sparrow. • The male house finch's plumage varies in colour from light yellow to bright red, but females will choose to breed with the reddest males. **Where found:** disturbed areas, including farms, ranches and towns; open fields and woodlands. *Winter:* backyard feeders; common year-round in southern ⅓ of B.C., becoming rare northward.

House Sparrow

Passer domesticus

Length: 14–17 cm
Wingspan: 24 cm

A black mask and bib adorn the male of this adaptive, aggressive species. • This abundant and conspicuous bird was introduced to North America in the 1850s as part of a plan to control the insects that were damaging grain and cereal crops. As it turns out, this species is largely vegetarian and usually feeds on seeds and grain! It also frequents fast-food restaurant parking lots, backyard bird feeders and farms. **Where found:** any human environment; common year-round in southern ⅔ of province, absent from central north coast.

AMPHIBIANS & REPTILES

A mphibians and reptiles are commonly referred to as cold blooded, but this term is misleading. Although reptiles and amphibians lack the ability to generate internal body heat, they are not necessarily cold blooded. These animals are ectothermic or poikilothermic, meaning that the temperature of the surrounding environment governs their body temperature. The animal will obtain heat from sunlight, warm rocks and logs, and warmed earth. Amphibians and reptiles hibernate in winter in cold regions, and some species of reptiles estivate (are dormant during hot or dry periods) in summer in hot regions. Both amphibians and reptiles moult (shed their skins) as they grow to larger body sizes.

Amphibians are smooth skinned and most live in moist habitats. They are represented by the salamanders, toads and frogs. These species typically lay shell-less eggs in jelly-like masses in water. The eggs hatch into gilled larvae, which later metamorphose into adults with lungs and legs. Amphibians can regenerate their skin and sometimes even entire limbs. Male and female amphibians often differ in size and colour, and males may have other specialized features when sexually mature, such as the vocal sacs in many frogs and toads.

Reptiles are completely terrestrial vertebrates with scaly skin. In this guide, the representatives are turtles, lizards and snakes. Most reptiles lay eggs buried in loose soil, but some snakes and lizards give birth to live young. Reptiles do not have a larval stage.

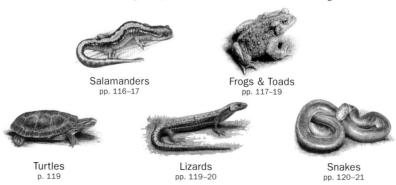

Salamanders
pp. 116–17

Frogs & Toads
pp. 117–19

Turtles
p. 119

Lizards
pp. 119–20

Snakes
pp. 120–21

Rough-skinned Newt

Taricha granulosa
Length: 12–20 cm

Newts hatch from eggs and begin their lives as tadpole-like aquatic larvae that spend 1–2 years in ponds, depending on local climate. In late summer, newly metamorphosed newts move into forested areas where they spend much of their lives in or under logs, only returning to water to breed. • The tough rough-skinned newt is found farther north than any other salamander in North America, even reaching the Alaskan frontier. **Where found:** moist, coastal forests, near water.

Northwestern Salamander

Ambystoma gracile
Length: 14–22 cm

Few people ever see these secretive but fascinating animals. They live in various forested habitats, consuming terrestrial invertebrates, occasionally wandering about on rainy nights. With the first warm spring rains, Ambystomids stage a mass migration to favoured breeding pools, where they congregate to mate and lay eggs. • Equipped with glands that secrete a mild toxin, these native salamanders are able to avoid predators and survive where introduced bullfrogs and predatory fish have become established. • The related British Columbia salamander (*A. g. decorticatum*) has light-coloured flecks and occurs in northern B.C. **Where found:** dense, humid forests; central and southern coast and Vancouver Is.

Long-toed Salamander

Ambystoma macrodactylum
Length: 10–17 cm

These striking, secretive creatures often hide under rocks or decomposing logs. They feed on invertebrates and are active primarily at night. They are more easily seen in the rainy months of April and May, when they migrate to their breeding sites in silt-free ponds and lakes. Eggs laid singly or in clumps on rocks or vegetation take about 3 weeks to hatch. • The related tiger salamander (*A. tigrinum*) is found in the Okanagan Valley. **Where found:** arid, low-elevation sagebrush, valley wetlands and subalpine forests; throughout southern ⅔ of B.C.

Western Red-backed Salamander

Plethodon vehiculum

Length: 7–12 cm

The western red-backed salamander is found in tremendous concentrations in Goldstream Provincial Park, a few minutes from Victoria. Flipping over a log may reveal a hiding salamander; just be sure to flip carefully and return the log to its original place to keep important hiding spots intact. **Where found:** moist, forested habitats; Vancouver Is. and the Fraser Valley to Hope.

Coastal Tailed Frog

Ascaphus truei

Length: 3–5 cm

Frigid mountain streams do not deter these tough little frogs. They lay their eggs on the downstream side of large rocks in fast-flowing streams to prevent them from being swept away in the current, and the tadpoles fastidiously cling to rocks with their suction cup-like mouths. • The adults vary in colour from green to grey, brown or reddish brown. The "tail" is actually the male copulatory organ; these frogs are one of the very few frog species with internal fertilization. **Where found:** cold, fast-flowing mountain streams; central and southern coast.

Western Toad

Bufo boreas

Length: 6–12 cm

Touching a toad will not give you warts, but the western toad does have a way of discouraging our unwanted affections: when handled, it secretes a toxin from large parotid glands behind its eyes that acts to irritate the mouth of potential predators. • This grey, green or brown, large toad is a voracious predator of insects and other tasty invertebrates such as worms and slugs. **Where found:** near springs, streams, meadows and woodlands; throughout, except extreme northeast.

Bullfrog

Rana catesbeiana

Length: up to 20 cm

Bullfrogs are not native to British Columbia but have become established on Vancouver Is. as far as Campbell River and in the Lower Mainland. They have also been reported in the Okanagan. Bullfrogs are very large and long-living frogs, averaging a lifespan of 7–9 years with records in captivity of individuals living to 16 years. • Bullfrogs are predatory, eating anything they can swallow, including certain snakes and fish, and are incredibly prolific, making them a significant threat to native frog populations. **Where found:** warm, still, shallow, vegetated waters of lakes, ponds, rivers and bogs; southern B.C.

Columbia Spotted Frog

Rana luteiventris

Length: 5–9 cm

This commonly seen amphibian does not venture far from water but lives in a variety of habitats ranging from alpine tundra to sagebrush lands to forests. These frogs visit shallow wetlands during the warmer months, but in winter they retreat to deeper waters that do not freeze solid. In spring, female spotted frogs deposit free-floating clumps of jelly that may contain up to 1500 eggs! **Where found:** various freshwater habitats and forest types; throughout B.C., except northeast.

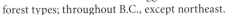

Wood Frog

Rana sylvatica

Length: 4.5 cm

Wood frogs are amphibians with anti-freeze. At below-zero temperatures, their heart rate, blood flow and breathing stop, turning them into froggy ice cubes. Special compounds, mainly glucose, allow them to survive partial freezing and thawing of their tissues. Thus, they are able to range north of the Arctic Circle, farther north than any other amphibian. • In early spring, when ice still fringes woodland pools, vernal wetlands explode to life as wood frogs invade to mate and lay eggs. Their collective calls sound like distant ducks quacking. **Where found:** moist woodlands, sometimes far from water; throughout, except extreme southwest and Vancouver Is.

Pacific Treefrog

Hyla regilla

Length: 3–5 cm

Pacific treefrogs have adhesive toe pads that enable them to climb vertical surfaces and cling to the tiniest branch. The frogs can also change colour within a few minutes, allowing them to blend into their immediate habitat. Colours include green, brown, grey, tan, reddish and black; dark spots are often present. Despite their name, they are often terrestrial, choosing moist, grassy habitat. **Where found:** low-elevation shrubby areas close to water; riparian areas; southern ½ of B.C.

Western Painted Turtle

Chrysemys picta

Length: 25 cm

Painted turtles can be seen basking in the sun on top of floating logs, mats of vegetation or exposed rocks. When alarmed, they slip into the water for a quick escape. • These turtles may live for up to 40 years. • There are 3 painted turtle subspecies, but only the largest, the western painted turtle, is found in our region. It has an olive-green carapace with red or orange underside borders. • The red-eared slider (*Trachemys scripta*), a turtle native to the southeastern U.S. and Mexico, has been introduced to Vancouver Is. and the Lower Mainland. **Where found:** marshes, ponds, lakes, slow-flowing streams; southern ⅓ of B.C.

Western Skink

Eumeces skiltonianus

Length: 15–18 cm

The juvenile western skink sports a bright blue tail that, when grabbed by predators, easily breaks off and continues to writhe while the skink makes its escape; it will soon grow a new tail. An adult's tail fades from blue, becoming reddish orange during breeding season. • Skinks feed on insects and spiders. **Where found:** among leaf litter and underneath bark and rocks; burrows in grasslands; various dry habitats of the Okanagan region.

Northern Alligator Lizard

Elgaria coerulea

Length: 15–25 cm

This skinny, fast-footed lizard may look like a miniature alligator but prefers dry land to swampy habitats. Wary of the open, the northern alligator lizard usually hides under rocks, logs or bark, occasionally emerging to bask in the sun. It lives in cool, shady forests and feeds on invertebrates. Females give birth to up to 8 live young. **Where found:** woodlands and forest clearings in southern B.C.

Rubber Boa

Charina bottae

Length: 35–80 cm

The rubbery appearance of this snake is owing to its small, smooth dorsal scales and soft, loose skin. It is sometimes called the "two-headed snake" because its head and the tip of its tail have the same thickness and colouring. • Like most constrictors, the rubber boa is an excellent climber and strangles its prey, which includes lizards, amphibians, birds and small mammals. Its defensive posture is to roll up into a ball, hiding its head. **Where found:** under logs or rocks; in grassy openings among trees in wooded areas and coniferous forests at lower elevations; southern ⅓ of B.C.

Yellow-bellied Racer

Coluber constrictor

Length: 60 cm–2 m

The racer relies on speed to catch prey and escape danger. On the ground, it moves with its head held high for a better view of the terrain; it will also climb shrubs to find birds and insects. • Certain individuals have a bluish caste to the body. The young have large, dark saddles on their backs and faint blotches on their sides. **Where found:** grasslands, savannah, rocky canyons; southern ⅓ of B.C.

Gophersnake

Pituophis catenifer

Length: 90 cm–3 m

This large, beautiful constrictor is often mistaken for a rattlesnake because of its similar colouration, patterning and aggressive defensive strategy. When threatened, it hisses and vibrates its tail against vegetation, often producing a rattling sound. • The gophersnake frequently overwinters in communal dens with other snakes, including rattlesnakes, gartersnakes and racers. **Where found:** open, dry, oak savannahs, brushy chaparral, meadows and sparse, sunny areas in coniferous forests and agricultural areas; southern ⅓ of B.C.

Common Gartersnake

Thamnophis sirtalis

Length: 40–100 cm

Probably our most commonly encountered snakes, gartersnakes can vary in colour but are normally prominently striped with alternating bands of yellow and dark. The red-sided subspecies has red markings along its sides. Terrestrial gartersnakes *(T. elegans)* and northwestern gartersnakes *(T. ordinoides)* are also found in southern B.C. • A female gartersnake can give birth to a litter of 3–83, but typically no more than 18, live young. **Where found:** meadows, marshes, gardens, suburban and urban areas; throughout, except northern B.C.

Western Rattlesnake

Crotalus viridus

Length: 60–100 cm

Our only venomous snake, the western rattlesnake warns away intruders by shaking the rattle at the tip of its tail. Those that ignore the warning risk a poisonous bite. A rattlesnake's deadly fangs are hinged and can be folded back into the mouth. • Western rattlesnakes are light brown or grey and blotched overall, with a triangular head, vertical pupils and special heat-sensing facial pits for locating warm-blooded prey. • During winter, rattlesnakes den communally in protected hibernacula such as abandoned animal burrows or rock crevices. **Where found:** dry, rocky areas with sparse tree cover; southern Interior of B.C.

FISH

Fish are ectothermic vertebrates that live in the water, have streamlined bodies covered in scales, and possess fins and gills. A fundamental feature of fish is the serially repeated set of vertebrae and segmented muscles that allows the animal to move from side to side, propelling it through the water. A varying number of fins, depending on the species, further aid the fish to swim and navigate. Most fish are oviparous and lay eggs that are fertilized externally. Eggs are either produced in vast quantities and scattered or they are laid in a spawning nest (redd) under rocks or logs. Parental care may be present in the defence of such a nest or territory. Spawning can involve migrating long distances from inland rivers where reproduction occurs, back to open waters such as the Pacific Ocean.

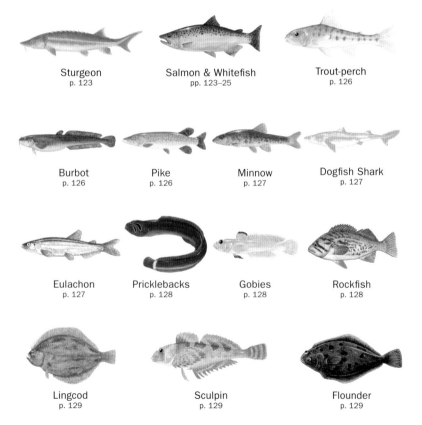

Sturgeon
p. 123

Salmon & Whitefish
pp. 123–25

Trout-perch
p. 126

Burbot
p. 126

Pike
p. 126

Minnow
p. 127

Dogfish Shark
p. 127

Eulachon
p. 127

Pricklebacks
p. 128

Gobies
p. 128

Rockfish
p. 128

Lingcod
p. 129

Sculpin
p. 129

Flounder
p. 129

White Sturgeon

Acipenser transmontanus

Length: 18 cm–2.3 m (max. 6.1 m)

For millions of years, the white sturgeon nosed along river bottoms, using the barbels around its mouth to detect prey. This relic has rows of hard plates called "scutes" running down its body. • Unfortunately, this species is now endangered because of overfishing in the 1900s, dams that have blocked migration routes and water pollution. • The white sturgeon can live up to 100 years and is the largest freshwater fish in North America. These giants will periodically rocket out of their deep river homes, hang motionless in the air for a split second, then crash back into the depths with a huge splash. **Where found:** landlocked population in large, cool rivers (Fraser R.) and large lakes; anadromous population mainly at sea but spawn inland.

Chinook Salmon

Oncorhynchus tshawytscha

Length: 84–91 cm

As the largest Pacific salmon, the chinook has rightfully earned the nickname "king salmon" by tipping the scales at a whopping 57 kg. Only ocean-going chinook grow this large; landlocked specimens remain much smaller because of a lack of suitable prey. • A single river can have several chinook runs during different seasons because of the species' variable spawning patterns. Generally, fish that migrate farther upstream turn up at the river mouth earlier. While some fish swim only short distances to spawn, others, such as the Fraser River chinook, may migrate 960 km or more. Depending on the food and habitat of the fish, the colour of its flesh may also vary from white to red. **Where found:** saltwater and freshwater habitats; western B.C.

Pink Salmon

Oncorhynchus gorbuscha

Length: 45–60 cm

Once considered undesirable, the importance of pink salmon or "humpies" has increased as other salmon stocks have declined. From June to September, adult pink salmon migrate up freshwater streams to spawning sites. The male develops a large hump on its back, an extended, turned-down snout and brighter colouring. The female lays up to 1900 orange-coloured eggs and guards them until she perishes, just days after spawning. Hatching occurs 3–4 months later and fry make their way downstream to the ocean. At 2 years of age, pinks return to the same river to begin the cycle again. **Where found:** mainly at sea but spawn inland.

123

Kokanee · Sockeye Salmon

Oncorhynchus nerka

Length: Kokanee: 20–35 cm; Sockeye: 55–65 cm

Named for the First Nations word for chief, "Sau-Kai," sockeye have always been valued along the Pacific Coast. They begin their 4-year lifecycle in freshwater streams, migrate to the Pacific Ocean, and then return to streams to spawn and die, providing an important food source for bears, eagles and other animals. Populations are in serious decline; theories attribute sea lice from farmed salmon, warming waters, changes to the food supply, or a combination of several factors. • Unlike anadromous sockeyes, smaller kokanees remain in freshwater for their entire lives. They occur naturally where sockeye no longer have access and have also been stocked in a number of cold, high-elevation lakes. **Where found:** saltwater and freshwater habitats.

Cutthroat Trout

Oncorhynchus clarki

Length: 25–38 cm (max. 1 m)

Named for the red streaking in the skin under the lower jaw, cutthroat trout seen in the water can be mistakenly identified as the similar-looking rainbow trout. The cutthroat's reddish belly and throat become brighter during spawning. Females excavate spawning nests (redds) with their tails in late spring or early summer. • There are several subspecies of cutthroat; some populations are coastal, others are freshwater residents and some travel between the brackish estuaries and the freshwater tributaries. **Where found:** saltwater and freshwater habitats; coastal regions and southeastern B.C.

Rainbow Trout

Oncorhynchus mykiss

Length: 30–46 cm (max. 92 cm)

Because of anglers' love of the rainbow trout, it has spread from western North America to 6 continents, becoming the most widely introduced species in the world. The trademark colourful appearance and heavily spotted back and sides vary in hue with lifestyle and habitat. • Rainbow trout in streams are bottom feeders but will often rise to the surface to leap for a struggling insect. They are highly respected by fly fishermen because of their spectacular jumps and fighting strength. **Where found:** cool, well-oxygenated waters; near swift currents in streams; throughout southern ⅔ of province. **Also known as:** steelhead trout, redband trout, silver trout.

Lake Trout

Salvelinus namaycush

Length: 45–65 cm (max. 1 m)

Large, solitary lake trout prefer ice-
cold water. In summer, they follow the retreat of
colder water to the bottom of a lake, rarely making excursions into the warm
surface layer. • Despite their slow growth, lake trout can reach old ages and large
sizes. Large trout are often over 20 years old, with one granddaddy of a specimen
reaching 62 years old! • Lake trout can take 6 years or more to reach maturity and
may spawn only once every 2–3 years, making recovery from overfishing difficult.
Where found: usually in deep, cooler lakes; throughout central and northern B.C.

Arctic Grayling

Thymallus arcticus

Length: 15–30 cm (max. 76 cm)

The arctic grayling's large dorsal
fin—the aquatic equivalent of deer
or moose antlers—and its vivid colouration
identify this species immediately. During spawning, this fish ventures from lakes
and large rivers to smaller tributaries, where each male aggressively defends its
selected spawning ground. • A fish of cold, clear streams, the arctic grayling is
vulnerable to changes in the environment. This fish needs to see its food to catch
it, so clean, clear water is vital. **Where found:** clear, cold waters of large rivers, rocky
creeks, lakes; northern B.C.

Mountain Whitefish

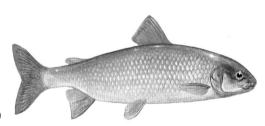

Prosopium williamsoni

Length: 15–45 cm (max. 58 cm)

This coldwater fish has endured habitat changes and increased fishing pressures
remarkably well. However, whitefish are sensitive to environmental or chemical
pollution and are sometimes likened to a canary in a coalmine. • Some mountain
whitefish can be sedentary, but many populations are known for their migratory
behaviour. In fact, mountain whitefish seem in perpetual migration between
seasonal feeding habitats and spawning grounds, and they move in large groups
from pool to pool. **Where found:** cold, deep lakes, rivers and large streams with
deep pools; throughout, except coastal areas.

Trout-perch

Percopsis omiscomaycus

Length: 7–10 cm (max. 13 cm)

Transparent skin makes trout-perch fascinating: you can peer straight through to the body cavity if you look carefully, and you can actually see the two huge otoliths (ear bones) lying alongside the brain. • An important prey species for larger fish such as lake trout and burbot, trout-perch hide under rocks and usually feed at night. • Shine a flashlight into the shallows on a dark June night and you may see the big eyes and chunky pale bodies of spawning trout-perch. They are one of the few non-salmonids with an adipose fin. **Where found:** usually deeper water, but spawns and feeds in shallows; restricted to northwestern B.C. but can be abundant where found.

Burbot

Lota lota

Length: 30–80 cm (max. 1 m)

The burbot is the only member of the cod family confined to freshwater. • The single chin barbel and the pectoral fins contain taste buds. As these fish grow, they satisfy their ravenous appetite for whitefish and suckers by eating larger fish instead of increased numbers of smaller ones, sometimes swallowing fish almost as big as themselves. A 30-cm-long walleye was found in the stomach of a large burbot. • Once considered by anglers to be a "trash" fish, the burbot is gaining popularity among sport fishers. **Where found:** bottom of cold lakes and rivers; east of Coastal Mountains.

Northern Pike

Esox lucius

Length: 46–76 cm (max. 133 cm; female is larger than male)

If you canoe, watch for adult pike hanging motionless among the reeds or along the edges of a dense aquatic plant bed. This carnivorous fish lies in wait of prey—usually young fish, but occasionally crayfish, frogs and even ducklings—then attacks with a quick stab of its long snout, clamping down on its victim with heavily toothed jaws. These predatory fish are at the top of the food chain and have a voracious appetite. When introduced to lakes where they do not normally occur, they can do considerable damage to the ecosystem. **Where found:** vegetated edges of warmer lakes and rivers; northeastern B.C. **Also known as:** jackfish, pickerel, water wolf.

Longnose Dace

Rhinichthys cataractae

Length: 5–9 cm (max. 13 cm)

This widely distributed minnow spends the daylight hours
under rocks, hiding from predators such as trout. At night, longnose dace emerge
to feed on aquatic insects and insect larvae. • Like most fishes that spend their
time in fast water, the longnose dace has a small swim bladder and a wedge-
shaped head that allows it to remain close to the bottom, even in fast-moving
waters. **Where found:** near the bottom of riffles in fast-flowing, cold streams; cold
lakes; throughout, except northwestern B.C.

Spiny Dogfish

Squalus acanthias

Length: 80–100 cm (max. 160 cm)

Fierce-looking dogfish are small,
schooling sharks that may dart toward divers with
unnerving speed. If captured, spiny dogfish can bend their back and puncture
their captor using their two dorsal spines, and then secrete a mild poison.
• Fossil records indicate that dogfish sharks date back 135 million years. Once
the world's most abundant sharks, spiny dogfish have declined dramatically
owing to overfishing. **Where found:** variety of habitats from shallow inshore
waters to great depths.

Eulachon

Thaleichthys pacificus

Length: 23 cm

Highly prized eulachon were trapped
and netted by First Nations peoples for centuries. These fish are so high in oil that
when dried and fitted with a wick, they can be used as a candle. The unique fish
oil is solid at room temperature, similar to soft butter. Eulachon were a vital
source of food and fat, and were also used as barter, along traditional "grease
trails" where they were traded to Interior peoples for animal skins or meat or
other necessities. **Where found:** Pacific Ocean, but return to freshwater rivers to
spawn, including Fraser, Skeena, Nass and Klinaklini rivers. **Also known as:**
oolichan, candlefish.

Black Prickleback

Xiphister atropurpureus

Length: up to 30 cm

Although it looks and acts similar to an eel, the black prickleback is not a true eel. It often slithers out of water to lie under rocks and seaweed, able to breathe air out of water for 10 hours or longer as long as it stays relatively moist. • The breeding pair fastidiously fertilizes each of their 738–4070 eggs individually, adding them one by one to a cluster! **Where found:** saltwater habitats; close to rocky shores with algal cover; tide pools, lower intertidal and shallow subtidal zones; under rocks and in gravel areas. **Also known as:** black blenny.

Blackeye Goby

Rhinogobiops nicholsii

Length: up to 15 cm

Frequently seen by sport divers, gobies have interesting colours and patterns and large eyes. The blackeye goby is less colourful than many other gobies, but it has distinctive black, bulbous eyes that contrast with its pale body. A black border to the dorsal fin (and pectoral fin of breeding males) is a diagnostic feature. • It lays 500–3000 eggs over the spawning season and is very territorial toward other blackeye gobies near its nest. **Where found:** saltwater habitats; sand- and mud-bottomed waters near rocky areas and reefs and in bays as well as in deep waters.

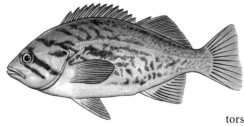

Blue Rockfish

Sebastes mystinus

Length: up to 53 cm

Significant numbers of these fish are claimed by sport fishing each year; their wild predators include seals and sea lions. Predation on eggs is reduced by female rockfish carrying the eggs internally until just before they are ready to hatch. • Blue rockfish are sometimes found in large groups feeding on jellyfish, smaller fish and crustaceans. They can also be found among rocky reefs, where they are a popular subject of underwater photographers; their sedentary behaviour makes it seem like they actually pose for the camera. **Where found:** saltwater habitats; rocky reefs in both shallow and deep waters; kelp beds.

Lingcod

Ophiodon elongatus

Length: up to 1.5 m

The largest lingcod recorded in B.C.
was 152 cm long and weighed in at
36.3 kg; the average weighs half that figure.
It is a highly prized sport-fish and a popular
food for humans and sea lions. • This spiny,
unfriendly looking fish is very territorial; males vigilantly guard nests containing
egg masses 60 cm across. **Where found:** saltwater habitats; seasonal migration
between shallow and deep waters to 2000 m. *Adult:* rocky reefs and kelp. *Juvenile:*
sandy or muddy bays.

Tidepool Sculpin

Oligocottus maculosus

Length: 7 cm

Sculpins are famous for their
looks—they're so ugly that they're cute.
Bulging eyes; fat, wide lips; roughly textured skin with
mottled colouration and dorsal spines add up to one visually
impressive fish. • An individual tidepool sculpin tends to select one particular
tide pool to call home and will return to it if displaced. **Where found:** saltwater
habitats; sheltered intertidal areas; tide pools.

Pacific Sanddab

Citharichthys sordidus

Length: up to 41 cm

The Pacific sanddab is a type
of flatfish that hides in the
sand at the seafloor. Its flat body and cryptic colouration keep this fish almost invisible with
only a thin layer of sand atop it. • Although born with an eye on either side of its
head, the Pacific sanddab spends its life lying on its right side, resulting in both
its eyes shifting to the left (top) side of its body (occasionally an individual will lie
to the other side). • In certain areas, such as California, it is a highly sought-after
fish commercially. **Where found:** saltwater habitats; soft, sandy ocean.

INVERTEBRATES

More than 95% of all animal species are invertebrates, and there are thousands of invertebrate species in our region. The few mentioned in this guide are frequently encountered and easily recognizable. Several aquatic species are included because exploring a pond with a bucket and dip net is a fun activity for children and a great way to introduce the concept of food chains. Invertebrates can be found in a variety of habitats and are an important part of most ecosystems. They provide food for birds, amphibians, shrews, bats and other insects, and they also play a vital role in the pollination of plants and aid in the decay process.

Seashells
pp. 132–34

Sea Slug
p. 134

Sea Cucumber
p. 134

Sea Stars
p. 135

Sand Dollar & Sea Urchin
pp. 135–36

Anemones, Coral & Sponge
pp. 136–37

Jellyfish
p. 137

Octopus
p. 138

Barnacles & Shrimp
p. 138

Crabs
p. 139

Butterflies & Moths
pp. 140–41

Dragonflies
p. 142

Beetles
p. 143

Wasps & Bees
p. 144

Ants
p. 144

Crane Flies & Lacewings
p. 145

Grigs
p. 145

Freshwater Aquatic
Invertebrates
p. 146

Centipede &
Millipede
p. 147

Spiders
p. 147

Mask Limpet

Tectura persona

Length: 3–5 cm

This large limpet is light adverse and hides from the sun and from bird predators, such as the black oystercatcher, by attaching to the undersides of boulders, overhangs, crevices or the roofs of sea caves. It is active at night when it moves about feeding on diatoms and other algae. **Where found:** upper and middle intertidal zone. **Also known as:** speckled, large variegated or inflated limpet.

Black Tegula

Tegula funebralis

Length: 2.5 cm

These snails are some of the most abundant on the Pacific Coast. Large individuals are known to live 20–30 years. They take advantage of sloped substrates to flee predators such as sea stars by pulling inside their shells and rolling away. • Empty black tegula shells are a favourite home acquisition of hermit crabs. **Where found:** rocky shores between high- and low-tide lines. **Also known as:** turban tegula, black turban snail.

Lewis' Moon Snail

Euspira lewisii

Length: 9 cm

The large, grey foot and mantle that covers most of its shell are characteristic of this large, almost round snail. • Lewis' moon snail preys on small clams it finds in the mud and feeds by wrapping its foot around them, drilling a hole into the clamshell with its radula and chewing out the contents. This method of feeding explains the small holes often found in clamshells that wash up on the beach. **Where found:** sand and sand-mud substrates; intertidal zones, sandy flats and bays with quiet waters.

Olympia Oyster

Ostrea lurida

Diameter: 2–5 cm

Native to our shores, the Olympia oyster is now a threatened species sensitive to over-harvesting, pollution, dredging and water temperature changes. It has suffered from being preyed upon by the oyster drill snail *(Cerateotoma inornatum)* and out-competed for its habitat by the giant Pacific oyster *(Crassostrea gigas)*, both introduced from Japan. • Olympia oyster is a culinary delicacy and is commercially farmed on a small scale. • Oysters are filter feeders and can change gender. **Where found:** attached to rocks in mud in the lower intertidal and shallow subtidal zones of sheltered saltwater lagoons and estuaries.

Pacific Razor Clam

Siliqua patula

Length: 18 cm

Prized by commercial fisheries, this clam is a favourite of seafood enthusiasts. Clam diggers do not have to dig deep to collect this mollusc, but they must be prepared to get wet. The Pacific razor clam does not dig a permanent burrow; instead, it moves about with the waves and continuously digs shallow holes in the sand until it is ready to catch the next good wave. • A razor clam can live 18 years, though it typically doesn't survive more than 5 years before being preyed upon. **Where found:** near the low-tide line and in shallow water all along the coast.

California Mussel

Mytilus californianus

Length: 26 cm

California mussels are the most conspicuous and abundant animals on our shores. They are predominant in the upper tidal zone and occur in massive growths. Mussels are capable of limited locomotion but rarely move from their practically permanent position; they attach to a substrate by byssal threads produced by their foot. • Sea stars, crabs, shorebirds and sea otters are among their top predators, but the supreme enthusiast for this tasty mollusc is human.
Where found: on rocks, wharf pilings and unprotected shores; from well above the low-tide line to water 25 m deep.

Lined Chiton

Tonicella lineata

Length: 5 cm

The gorgeous lined chiton sports an array of fashionable shells typically mottled reddish brown as a background and decorated with zigzag lines patterned across it in colours varying from light and dark reds to blues or browns to black or white. The fleshy girdle that surrounds the 8-sectioned plate of armour (chitons are the only mollusc with jointed shells) is usually a greenish or yellowish colour. **Where found:** on rocks covered with coralline algae; underneath purple sea urchins; from the low-tide line to depths of 55 m.

Sea Lemon

Anisodoris nobilis

Length: 26 cm

The sea lemon feeds entirely upon sponges. It has a fruity (lemony according to some) scent that is apparently repellent to predators. • Nudibranchs are poor swimmers; instead, they crawl along the ocean floor with a strong, suction-like foot common to all slug species of gastropods. • The sea lemon has 2 antenna-like rhinophores at its anterior end, a circular, many-branched cluster of gills on the posterior end and is covered in short, rounded tubercles everywhere in between. **Where found:** on pilings, around docks and on rocks below the low-tide line. **Also known as:** noble Pacific doris.

Red Sea Cucumber

Cucumaria miniata

Length: 26 cm

Typically bright red, but also orange, pink or purple, this long, smooth, highly tentacled sea cucumber nestles in crevices and under rocks within moving water currents. It has 10 main retractable tentacles of equal length, each highly branched at the ends, and 5 rows of tube feet along its length. • Sea cucumbers are detritivores, feeding on dead and decaying organic material. • As a defence mechanism, and no doubt effectively repulsive, sea cucumbers can spit out their guts and regenerate them. **Where found:** near the low-tide line and in shallow depths in circulating waters.

Blood Star

Henricia leviuscula

Diameter: max. 12 cm

Noticeable for its remarkable orange, red or purple colouring, the blood star sometimes has light pink blotches or dark banks. It is a delicate and graceful-looking sea star with a relatively small central disc and 4–6 long, tapering rays. It feeds mainly on sponges but will also prey upon bivalves, bryozoa, fish and even other sea stars. • Less common intertidally but one of our most beautiful sea stars, rose star *(Crossaster papposus)* has 8–14 (usually 13) rays and sharp spines covering its scarlet body. **Where found:** common in the rocky intertidal and subtidal zones; low intertidal to 670 m.

Ochre Sea Star

Pisaster ochraceus

Radius: 26 cm

Beautiful yellow, orange, brown, reddish or purple ochre sea stars often suffer from over-collection by beachcombers who unfortunately do not realize that the colour will be lost once the sea star dies and dries up. • Ochre sea stars are an important, keystone predatory species whose absence in an ecosystem causes visible shifts in the numbers, types and dominances of other species. This sea star is abundant on beds of mussels, its favoured prey, and is preyed upon by gulls and sea otters. • Variably coloured six-armed sea star *(Leptasterias hexactis)* is also very common under and on intertidal rocks. **Where found:** intertidal areas; wave-washed, rocky shores at the low-tide line.

Eccentric Sand Dollar

Dendraster excentricus

Radius: 4 cm

Beachcombers are most familiar with this sand dollar as a smooth, spineless, grey specimen with a 5-petaled flower design in the centre of its surface; in its living form, it is furry in appearance and its colour varies from light lavender-grey to brown or reddish brown to a dark, almost black, purple. • Eccentric sand dollars colonize sandy ocean floors, stabilizing the strata. In rough waters, they will bury themselves under the sand for protection. • Sand dollars are closely related to sea urchins. **Where found:** sandy bottoms of sheltered bays and open coasts; from the low-tide line to depths of 40 m.

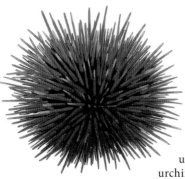

Purple Sea Urchin

Strongylocentrotus purpuratus

Radius: 5 cm without spines

In large populations, the purple sea urchin and the red sea urchin (*S. franciscanus*) are capable of overgrazing and destroying the important kelp forests, a situation that a healthy population of sea otters, the urchin's main predator, keeps in check. Sea urchins, sea otters and kelp forests maintain a tight interrelationship and all require unpolluted waters. • Adult purple sea urchins are a vivid purple, but the juveniles are green. **Where found:** from the low-tide line and rocky shores into kelp forests in waters up to 90 m deep.

Aggregating Anemone

Anthopleura elegantissima

Height: *Aggregating individuals:* 15 cm; *Solitary individuals:* 50 cm
Width: *Aggregating individuals:* 7.5 cm; *Solitary individuals:* 25 cm

This sea anemone has 5 rings of tentacles with tips varying in delicate colours of pink, lavender and blue. The aggregating form is in fact a colony of clones created by the "founding" anemone dividing itself in a form of asexual reproduction. These clones tolerate proximity to each other because they do not compete genetically; if a genetically different individual was in proximity, they would lash out with their tentacles, wounding or killing it. Their toxins are completely benign to their clones. **Where found:** rock walls, boulders or pilings from intertidal to low-tide zones.

Giant Green Anemone

Anthoplerua xanthogrammica

Height: 30 cm
Width: 25 cm

The giant green anemone is a solitary green giant, but it is not antisocial; often within tentacle-tip distance to another, it makes contact periodically as if to reassure itself that it is not alone. • Its green column varies to brown, and its thick, short, tapered tentacles vary from green to blue to white in rows of 6 or more. The green colouring is enhanced by a symbiotic relationship with green algae and protists, from which the anemone obtains photosynthetic by-products. **Where found:** exposed coastlines; on rocks, seawalls and pilings in tide pools and to depths of more than 15 m.

Orange Cup Coral

Balanophyllia elegans

Height: 1.25 cm
Width: 1.25 cm

This is the only stony coral in the intertidal
zone of the Pacific coast from British Columbia
to Baja California. Stony coral has a stony, cup-
shaped skeleton in which the base of the animal is set,
and 36 long, tapered, translucent tentacles that reach out and contract back within the
skeleton. The tentacles have masses of stinging cells dotted along them, so do not be
tempted to touch this lovely, bright orange beauty. The fluorescent pigment is bright
even at depths of 9 m or more. **Where found:** shaded waters such as under ledges and
boulders from the low-tide line down to depths of 21 m; all along the coast.

Bread Crumb Sponge

Halichondria panicea

Thickness: to 5.1 cm

This encrusting sponge has a breadcrumb-like texture
and can be found in various colours, from yellow to
green. It often takes on a blue to greenish tint from
a symbiotic relationship with a microscopic algae called
zoochlorellae. • Sponges reproduce either by budding (a tip is
released or breaks off and regenerates upon attachment to a new site) or by releasing
tiny clusters of cells that germinate on a new site. • When broken apart or dead and
decaying, this sponge gives off an odour that some compare to sulphur or ignited
gunpowder. **Where found:** common in shady areas of tide pools and under rock
overhangs on low intertidal rocks, and subtidally.

Moon Jellyfish

Aurelia aurita

Radius: 19 cm

This ethereal, whitish to translucent
medusa is a favourite food of the leath-
erback sea turtle but is not a favoured
acquaintance of swimmers and
snorkellers—a jellyfish can give a painful sting, and it also releases polyps in the
water that are very difficult to see but easily felt. The sting may cause a slight rash or
itching for several hours. • The moon jellyfish has 8 lobes fringed by numerous
short tentacles and 4 long oral arms, also with frilly margins. **Where found:** floats
near the surface just offshore and often washes up on beaches during high tide or
after a storm.

137

North Pacific Giant Octopus

Enteroctopus dolfeini

Armspread: average 4.3 m to over 9 m

North Pacific giant octopus is one of the largest octopods anywhere in the world, weighing on average 15–40 kg but on scientific record up to 71 kg and unconfirmed records at over 250 kg. • Extremely advanced invertebrates that possess many clever behaviours, octopi are a constant source of entertainment for divers and snorkellers; their ability to squirt screens of ink and change the colour and texture of their skin to camouflage against their surroundings are among the most impressive. **Where found:** sandy habitats in shallow waters close to shore, out to typical depths of 65 m, but can be found in deeper waters to 750 m.

Giant Acorn Barnacle

Balanus nubilus

Radius: up to 5 cm

We typically see this barnacle closed, but when it feeds (rarely and sometimes not for months at a time), long, feathery plumes reach out from the top of the barnacle shell to filter bits of organic matter from the water. • This barnacle is intolerant of exposure and must remain almost continuously covered by water, or it will easily desiccate. • Capable of sexual reproduction yet immobile, this animal has the largest penis-to-body size ratio so that the male can reach his mate. **Where found:** rocky shores and exposed coasts; lower intertidal areas with continuous water cover; subtidal to depths of 91 m.

Barred Shrimp

Heptacarpus pugettensis

Length: up to 2.5 cm

Heptacarpus species are the "broken-back" shrimps, named for the distinctive kink in their backs. Many species in quite high numbers are along our coast, but they are not often noticeable while they lay motionless in bright daylight hours, their translucent colouring blending them into the substrate. Disturb still tide pool waters and watch them scurry. **Where found:** from the low-tide line to depths of 15 m.

Dungeness Crab

Cancer magister

Length: 16.5 cm

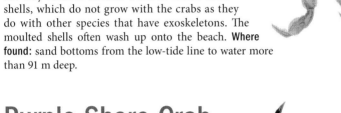

These crabs are the most sought-after species for commercial harvest on the Pacific Coast south of Alaska. Dungeness crabs are usually only found in water around 30 m deep, but they come to shallow water to moult their shells, which do not grow with the crabs as they do with other species that have exoskeletons. The moulted shells often wash up onto the beach. **Where found:** sand bottoms from the low-tide line to water more than 91 m deep.

Purple Shore Crab

Hemigrapsus nudus

Length: 5 cm

The purple shore crab scuttles sideways about rocky shorelines scavenging animal matter and grazing on the film of algae growing on the rocks. It hides under rocks and burrows under mud for shelter and is quite tolerant of remaining dry for extended periods without desiccating. **Where found:** open, rocky shores; among seaweeds in shallow, protected waters.

Blue-handed Hermit Crab

Pagurus samuelis

Length: 2 cm

The blue-handed hermit crab does not produce its own shell, and only the front portion of its body is armoured; it must protect the soft regions of its body by acquiring a discarded snail shell. The black tegula shell is one of the preferred shells for this little crab to make a home. If the crab outgrows its current shell or finds a more suitable and otherwise unoccupied shell, it will relocate. **Where found:** open, rocky shores; permanent tide pools; from the intertidal zone subtidal to depths of 15 m.

Anise Swallowtail

Papilio zelicaon

Wingspan: 60–95 mm

The "tail" of the swallowtail is defensive; the strategy is that attacking birds will grab at this extension, in which event the butterfly's body will be spared. This butterfly is often seen with the lower half of its wings missing, implying that the strategy must indeed work. • The swallowtail never seems to go unnoticed or without a compliment from its observer. The caterpillar is also attractive, sporting a smooth, green, black and yellow body. **Where found:** sunny habitats in gardens, meadows and hilltops throughout B.C.

Spring Azure

Celastrina lucia

Wingspan: 28–30 mm

This dainty, blue butterfly is one of the first butterflies to announce the arrival of spring. It feeds on the buds and flowers of spring blooms on mountain shrubs. An adult lives for only 1–2 weeks, in which time it must breed and lay its eggs. The larvae often develop on the leaves of dogwood and cherry trees and may be tended to and protected by ants for the sweet "honeydew" that they produce. **Where found:** lush valley bottoms, meadows, open forests, shrubby areas and along rivers and streams.

Clouded Sulphur

Colias philodice

Wingspan: 35–55 mm

Differing from each other mainly in colour between yellow and orange, the many species of sulphur are all very tricky to tell apart. • Like all other butterflies, sulphurs play a vital role in pollinating many wild plants. Attracted to flowers by their brilliantly coloured petals, butterflies obtain nectar with their long, coilable proboscis and meanwhile are sprinkled with fine, sticky pollen, which they carry to the next plant. **Where found:** meadows, fields and vegetated roadsides; from low-elevation valleys to subalpine areas.

Pacific Fritillary

Boloria epithore

Wingspan: 40 mm

Fritillaries are a group of orange and black butterflies. Lesser fritillaries, such as the Pacific fritillary, are smaller than the greater fritillaries and do not have the greaters' typical silver spots on their underwings. • Lesser fritillaries are noticeable for spreading their wings while they feed, rather than folding them atop their backs. For this reason, lessers are favourite subjects for nature photographers. **Where found:** meadows and coniferous forests. **Also known as:** western meadow fritillary.

Mourning Cloak

Nymphalis antiopa

Wingspan: 50–80 mm

One of the longest-living butterflies, mourning cloaks live up to a full year—most butterflies live mere days or weeks, rarely months—and are tolerant of cool temperatures. Adults emerge from their pupae in mid- to late summer and may over-winter under bark, debris or even a window shutter, but if temperatures are above freezing, they can be seen even in winter. They emerge from hibernation in spring to mate and lay eggs. • The caterpillars feed with enthusiasm on willow trees. **Where found:** openings in forested areas.

Polyphemus Moth

Antheraea polyphemus

Wingspan: 110 mm

This large moth is always noticed for its spectacular colours and designs. The large eyespots exist for defensive purposes; if the wings are closed and a predator, such as a bird, approaches, the polyphemus moth will flash its wings open like eyelids to create the illusion that it is a much larger creature and not prey. • Polyphemus was a one-eyed giant in Greek mythology. **Where found:** southern deciduous forests.

Common Spreadwing

Lestes disjunctus

Length: 35 mm

As an exception to the rule about how dragonflies and damselflies posture their wings, this damselfly assumes the dragonfly position, thus giving it the name spreadwing. Juveniles have a bit of blue colouring, but as the common spreadwing ages, it becomes iridescent green or brown and is covered in a waxy powder called pruinose that is very much like the waxiness of a plum or prune. Specialists theorize that pruinose adds to the reflectivity of the ultraviolet signals that this insect uses in courtship. **Where found:** in ponds and lakes and near slow-flowing streams throughout B.C.

American Emerald

Cordulia shurtleffi

Length: 45 mm

The American emerald is a beautiful dragonfly of the northern forests. The large, bright green eyes are vivid against its dark, iridescent, coppery jade body. It comes out in large numbers in the boggy forests in spring to breed and lay its eggs. **Where found:** quiet, still waters of boggy ponds, marshes and shallow lakes, throughout B.C.

Cherry-faced Meadowhawk

Sympetrum internum

Length: 35 mm

The little red or yellow dragonflies common in parks and gardens are the meadowhawks. The cherry-faced meadowhawk is one of the most common species: males have a cherry-red face and a deep red body; females or young males are yellowish. • Dragonflies breed in ponds, but meadowhawks will wander far from water to feed. You can sneak up and get a good look at them, because they often perch on or close to the ground. **Where found:** ponds and lakes; prefer stagnant waters, throughout B.C.

Mountain Pine Beetle

Dendroctonus ponderosae

Length: 5 mm

Population outbreaks of this high-profile
beetle have destroyed hundreds of thousands of hectares of pine forests (mainly
lodgepole and ponderosa pine). The beetles
attack old or dying trees, and early stages of
infestations occur when trees are in overcrowded,
poor site conditions or are otherwise stressed by root
disease or fire damage. Clear-cutting practices create even-aged stands in crowded
situations inviting outbreaks, which, when severe enough, can spread even to
healthy stands. The beetle bores into and destroys the phloem layer, thus cutting off
nutrients to the tree. **Where found:** pine forests of Interior B.C.

Spruce Sawyer

Monochamus scutellatus

Length: 20 mm, plus long antennae

Finding this miniature replica of the
Asian longhorn beetle in your backyard is a thrill. The exotic-looking
spruce sawyer has a white-flecked
ebony body and long, curved antennae.
These marvellous beasts pupate inside dead spruce trees, and
the larvae hollow out winding galleries through the wood. When the awkward,
noisy adults emerge to mate, they fly with their bodies held vertically and their
legs sticking out in all directions. **Where found:** forests throughout B.C.

Two-spot Ladybug

Adalia bipunctata

Length: 4 mm

This native ladybug is variable in appearance, typically displaying the two spots of its
name; however, some may have four spots and
some are almost all black with only red shoulders.
They emerge from the pupae and do not change their
size or the number of spots as they age. • Ladybugs,
which feed ravenously on aphids, can be bought in garden centres to put into a
garden with aphid problems; they will have a significant impact, especially in
a greenhouse. Once released, most will fly away. **Where found:** trees, shrubs and
buildings throughout B.C.

Yellow Jacket

Vespula spp.

Length: 10–15 mm

Amazing engineers of paper architecture, yellow jackets chew on bark or wood and mix it with saliva to make the pulp. Large sheets of paper line the nest in which 6-sided paper chambers hold the larvae. Different types of wood create swirls of colour, greys and browns, inadvertently adding some artistic style to the structure. The nest can reach the size of a basketball by the end of summer; only the queen, however, will survive winter—the only safe time of year to get a close-up look at a wasp nest without being stung by one of these ill-tempered hornets. **Where found:** nest in high branches or in abandoned animal burrows; widespread.

Bumble Bee

Bombus spp.

Length: 10–20 mm

These large, fuzzy bees are intimidating but not aggressive, and they can be closely approached. Their dense, hairy coats help warm them, and "bumbles" can often fly in cooler weather than many other insects. Their hairy coats also make them extremely effective pollinators; as they visit flowers, the pollen adheres readily to their "fur" and is transferred to other plants.
• Bumble bees usually build nests in underground burrows, and only young queens survive winter to start new colonies the next spring. **Where found:** clearings and meadows wherever there are flowering plants; throughout.

Carpenter Ant

Camponotus spp.

Length: 12 mm

Woe to homeowners with a colony of these woodborers in their houses. Carpenter ants damage the wooden infrastructure of a home. Small tunnels, or galleries, with occasional slit-like openings where the ants expel sawdust, characterize their presence. The ants don't actually eat the wood, as do termites; they are making nests. Carpenter ants do best in wood with 15% or higher moisture content.
• In the wild, they excavate trees and form extensive galleries. Large pileated woodpeckers (*Dryocopus pileatus*) readily tune into these colonies and often rip apart large sections of bark to get at the ants. **Where found:** forested areas throughout B.C.

Giant Crane Fly

Holorusia spp.

Length: up to 25 cm

These innocent insects are not giant mosquitoes or garden harvestmen ("daddy longlegs") but very benign and harmless crane flies. Giant crane flies do not bite, and their larvae only scavenge in soil and rotting logs. • The crane is an appropriate analogy to these long-legged creatures that are more comfortable in the forest than when they accidentally find themselves inside your house. **Where found:** forested areas throughout B.C.

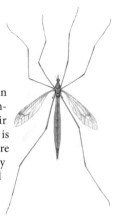

Green Lacewing

Chrysopa spp.

Length: 10 mm

Lacewings are frequent visitors to your garden, where their lime-green bodies camouflage with the light foliage of young plants. They have elegant filigreed wings (hence lacewing), large golden eyes and, if you pick one up, you will notice they produce an odd scent. • Both the adults and larvae of these beneficial insects feed on aphids. **Where found:** shrubby or forested areas and gardens; widespread.

Cave Cricket

Ceuthophilus spp.

Length: about 12 mm

Cave crickets need a dark moist environment, making some people associate them with cockroaches, which they are not. They do not have wings and, therefore, though they are crickets, they cannot chirp. They feel their way through their dark environment with long antennae. **Where found:** in rodent burrows, under rocks or in rotten wood; rarely in caves but sometimes in house basements; widespread throughout B.C. **Also known as:** camel cricket, owing to its humped back.

Water Boatman

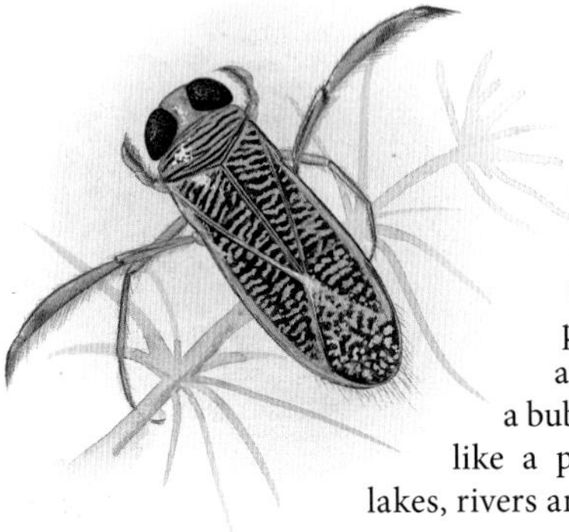

Family Corixidae

Length: 4–10 mm

The three sets of legs on the water boatman are each adapted for a specific function: digging in the mud for food, holding on to plants and rocks underwater, or swimming and maneuvring. These great divers carry a bubble of air under their abdomens to use much like a primitive scuba tank. **Where found:** ponds, lakes, rivers and streams throughout B.C.

Pond Skater

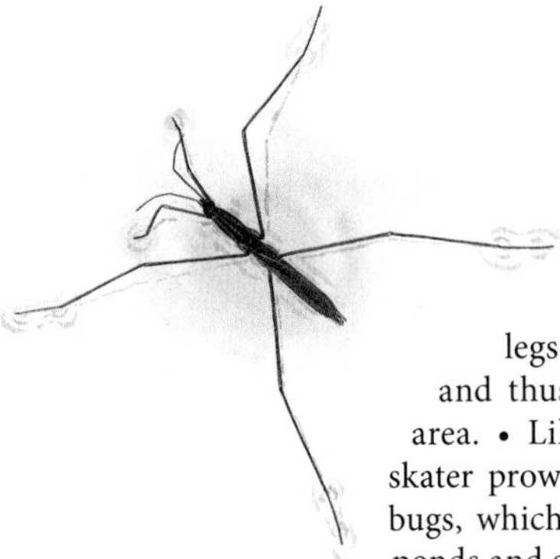

Limnoporus notabilis

Length: up to 20mm

Surface tension on water along with the body shape of this insect allows the kayak pond skater to walk, or skate, on water. Its legs are water repellent, long and far-reaching, and thus distribute the skater's weight over a large area. • Like a diligent pool cleaner, the kayak pond skater prowls the water's surface for dead or drowning bugs, which it quickly consumes. **Where found:** streams, ponds and small rivers throughout B.C.

Mayfly Larva

Order Ephemeroptera

Length: up to 30 mm

There are many species of mayfly that all generally live a single day in adult form. In larval form, however, they last a while longer if not eaten by one of their many aquatic predators. When they emerge as adults, they first go through a unique stage where they are called "duns" or "subimagos" before they once again shed their skin as well as their wings and become true adults that live only long enough to mate and lay eggs. **Where found:** fresh water habitats throughout B.C.

Garden Centipede

Lithobius spp.

Length: up to 30 mm

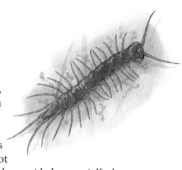

A centipede moves its many legs very quickly, but if you manage to see one sitting still, you can count 1 set of legs per body segment—significantly fewer than 100 feet, as the name would suggest. • This predator has venomous fangs with which it subdues its prey. It is not dangerous to people but nevertheless should be avoided, especially by small children. • Centipedes require a moist environment to survive and will quickly desiccate if they find their way into a house. **Where found:** under moist debris or cover in gardens and forests throughout B.C.

Cyanide Millipede

Harpaphe haydeniana

Length: 45 mm

Although it has twice as many legs as the centipede (2 sets per body segment), the millipede actually moves quite slowly. Because it feeds upon plants and detritus, the cyanide millipede does not need to move quickly to catch a meal. Its main defence against those animals that would want to prey upon it, such as birds and lizards, is to curl up in a ball and produce cyanide, which has an odour that deters a would-be predator. Some people compare the scent produced by this millipede to almond. **Where found:** forested areas of southern coastal B.C. **Also known as:** clown millipede, yellow-spotted millipede, almond-scented millipede.

Western Black Widow

Latrodectus hesperus

Length: *Male:* up to 5 mm; *Female:* up to 12 mm

Not known for its web-making skills, the black widow makes a disorganized mass of webs and lives in the abandoned burrows of small mammals. If seen out of hiding, the western black widow is easy to identify by its shiny, large, black body with a red hourglass on the underside. • It is fairly common knowledge that the bite of a black widow is dangerous and best avoided. Also accurate in common knowledge is that the female often eats the male after mating, but it is not the only spider to do so. **Where found:** dry, well-drained areas in southern B.C.

147

PLANTS

Plants belong to the Kingdom Plantae. They are autotrophic, which means they produce their own food from inorganic materials through a process called photosynthesis. Plants are the basis of all food webs. They supply oxygen to the atmosphere, modify climate and create soil and hold it in place. They disperse their seeds and pollen through carriers such as wind, water and animals. Fossil fuels come from ancient deposits of organic matter—largely that of plants. In this book, plants are separated into 3 categories: trees and tall shrubs; shrubs and vines; and forbs, ferns and grasses.

TREES

Trees are long-lived, woody plants that are normally taller than 6 metres. There are 2 types of trees in B.C.: coniferous and broadleaf. Conifers, or cone-bearers, have needles or small, scale-like leaves. Most conifers are evergreens, but some, such as larches (*Larix* spp.), shed their leaves in winter. Most broadleaf trees lose their leaves in autumn and are often called deciduous trees (meaning "falling off" in Latin). B.C. has one broadleaf tree that doesn't lose its leaves in autumn: arbutus (p. 157). This book gives measurements for average height trees in B.C., but some trees may reach greater heights.

A single tree can provide a home or a food source for many different animals. Roots bind soil and play host to a multitude of beneficial fungi, and even support certain semi-parasitic plants such as Indian paintbrush. Trunks provide a substrate for numerous species of moss and lichen, which in turn are used by many animals for shelter and nesting material. Tree cavities are used by everything from owls to squirrels to snakes. Leafy canopies support an amazing diversity of life. Myriad birds depend on mature trees, as do scores of insects. Both the seed cones of coniferous trees and the fruit of deciduous trees are consumed by all manner of wildlife.

A group of trees can provide windbreak, camouflage or shelter, and can hold down soil, thus preventing erosion. Streamside (riparian) woodlands are vital to protecting water quality. Their dense root layers filter out sediments and other contaminants that would otherwise enter watercourses. It is no mystery why Canada's healthiest rivers are also those that have abundant, undisturbed woodlands alongside them. There are many types of forest communities, and the types of soils on which they occur largely dictate their species composition. To some extent, the types of trees within a forest control what other species of plants and animals are present. Old-growth forest is critical habitat for many species that use the fallen or hollowed-out trees as nesting or denning sites. Many species of invertebrates live within or under the bark, providing food for birds. Fallen, decomposing logs provide habitat for snakes, salamanders, mosses, fungi and invertebrates. The logs eventually completely degrade into soil to perpetuate the continued growth of plant life and retain organic matter in the ecosystem. Large forests retain carbon dioxide, helping to reduce global warming. One giant old-growth tree can extract 7 kg of airborne pollutants annually and put back 14 kg of oxygen. Responsibly managed forests can also sustain an industry that provides wood products and jobs.

Pine
pp. 150–55

Yew
p. 155

Cedar
pp. 156–57

Heath
p. 157

Cottonwood & Aspen
p. 158

Birch
p. 159

Oak
p. 160

Dogwood
p. 160

Maple
p. 161

Rose
p. 161

White Spruce

Picea glauca

Height: 25–40 m
Needles: 1.5–2 cm long; stiff, 4-sided
Seed cones: 2.5–3.5 cm long; cylindrical, pale brown

Small white spruce often grow beneath old lodgepole pines. This species can live for 200 years and eventually replaces pines in mature forests. It is a good choice for landscaping and is used in reforestation. • Spruce needles roll between your fingers, unlike the flat, 2-sided needles of most other conifers. • This tree is an important source of food and shelter for many forest animals, including grouse and seed-eating birds, porcupines and red squirrels. • Related Engelmann spruce *(P. engelmannii)* grows on the mountain slopes of Interior B.C. **Where found:** various soils and climates, but prefers moist, rich soil; throughout, except coastal and southern areas.

Black Spruce

Picea mariana

Height: up to 15 m (rarely up to 30 m)
Needles: 0.5–1.0 cm long; stiff, 4-sided
Seed cones: 2–3 cm long; dull greyish brown to purplish brown

This slow-growing wetland tree, which may live for 200 years, is an important source of lumber and pulp. • Northern explorers used black spruce to make spruce beer, a popular drink that prevented scurvy. Spruce gum was also chewed or boiled into cough syrup to relieve sore throats (spruce should be used in moderation). • Snowshoe hares love to eat young spruce seedlings and red squirrels harvest the cones, but in general, black spruce is not favoured as a wildlife food source. • Many black spruce have a club-shaped crown. **Where found:** cool, damp, boggy sites in central and northern B.C.

Sitka Spruce

Picea sitchensis

Height: average 55 m; up to 95 m
Needles: 2–3 cm long; 4-sided, sharp
Seed cones: 5–10 cm long; reddish brown to brown

These very large trees are found along the B.C. Coast range, with the most majestic occurring on river floodplains. • Carmanah Walbran Provincial Park on Vancouver Is. is home to Canada's tallest tree, the 95-m tall Carmanah Giant. This 400-year-old Sitka spruce measures 9.4 m around. • Sitka spruce was used to make aircraft frames during World War II. **Where found:** moist, well-drained sites such as inlets and riparian areas; along Pacific coast fog belt to 500 m elevations.

Western White Pine

Pinus monticola

Height: up to 50 m
Needles: 5–10 cm long, in bundles of 5
Seed cones: 10–30 cm long, cylindrical, yellow-green to purple (young), reddish brown and woody (mature)

This lovely large pine is not as abundant in the wild as would be expected because of an introduced fungus that quickly kills young trees. White pine blister rust was brought in by imported eastern white pines. Non-resinous, soft and workable, western white pine wood is popular for mouldings, trim and handicrafts. • Whitebark pine *(P. albicaulis)*, found from 1000 m to treeline in the mountains of the Interior, is characterized by whitish bark and often multiple stems. **Where found:** moist valleys to open dry slopes; sea level to subalpine; southern B.C.

Ponderosa Pine

Pinus ponderosa

Height: up to 45 m
Needles: 12–25 cm long, in bundles of 3
Seed cones: 7–15 cm long, cylindrical;
scales tipped with stiff prickles

These stately pines thrive in areas that are periodically burned. Thick bark makes ponderosa pine fire resistant. • The straight, cinnamon-coloured trunks are distinctive, with black fissures outlining a jigsaw puzzle of thick plates of bark. • Native peoples ground the oil-rich seeds into meal and collected the sweet inner bark in spring, when the sap was running. Large scars can still be seen on some older trees, attesting to people's fondness for this sweet treat. **Where found:** mountains and steppe; southern Interior B.C.

Lodgepole Pine

Pinus contorta var. *latifolia*

Height: up to 30 m
Needles: 3–7 cm long, in pairs
Seed cones: 3–6 cm long, oval-shaped,
at right angles to branch or pointing back

Lodgepole pines are the first conifers to colonize areas burned by fire in Interior B.C. The cones are held shut with a tight resin bond that melts when heated, allowing the seeds to disperse. • Two closely related *P. contorta* varieties are found in B.C. Lodgepole pine, the tall, straight inland variety, was traditionally used to support tepees or to build lodges and is an important source of timber today. Mountain pine beetle outbreaks are a serious problem, killing large stands. • Short and scrubby shore pine (var. *contorta*) thrive along the coast, where salty sea spray and ocean winds cause twisted, stunted growth. **Where found:** (var. *latifolia*) variety of habitats, from dry sites to bogs; throughout Interior B.C.

Subalpine Fir

Abies lasiocarpa

Height: 20–30 m
Needles: 2–4 cm long; bluish-green, flattened, usually blunt
Seed cones: 5–10 cm; erect, barrel-shaped

Small subalpine fir needles have 2 white lines on the lower surface. Erect, deep-purple, barrel-shaped cones usually grow on upper branches, near the tree's spire-like crown. • The fragrance of these resinous evergreens often permeates the air near treeline. In sheltered valleys the spire-like crowns can reach their maximum height, but on high, exposed slopes, trees grow stunted and twisted like bonsai. • The oil-rich seeds are eaten by many species of birds, porcupines and squirrels. • Rocky Mountain fir *(A. bifolia)* shares similar habitat and is very similar in appearance but occurs in the eastern half of Interior B.C., including the Rocky Mountains. **Where found:** montane to subalpine; western half of Interior B.C.

Amabilis Fir

Abies amabilis

Height: up to 50 m
Needles: 2–3 cm long; flat; dark, shiny green above
Seed cones: 9–14 cm long; erect, deep purple, barrel-shaped

Along the B.C. coast, this shade-tolerant tree is often found in the forest understorey, growing with hemlocks, Sitka spruce and redcedar. Grand fir *(A. grandis)* has needles arranged in 2 clear rows, and grows with Douglas-fir in drier, rainshadow sites of eastern Vancouver Is., the Sunshine Coast and Okanagan. • Fir trees had many traditional uses: needles were burned as incense (smudging), boughs were used to line eulachon ripening pits, and resin was used to waterproof canoe seams. The wood was carved into canoe paddles, canoes and insect-proof storage boxes. **Where found:** moist, well-drained soils from sea level to subalpine on B.C. coast.

Western Larch

Larix occidentalis

Height: up to 50 m
Needles: 2–5 cm long; soft, deciduous
Seed cones: 2–3 cm long; oval when closed, egg-shaped when open

The leaves of this slender tree are unusual among conifers: they turn golden yellow and drop in autumn. They grow on stubby twigs in tightly spiraled tufts of 15–30. The seed cones have long, slender bract tips that extend beyond the scales. • Western larch is our largest larch. Thick bark helps mature trees to survive fires, and some live for 700–900 years. • The sap contains a natural sugar gelatin, said to taste like bitter honey, and hardened pitch can be chewed like gum. **Where found:** gravelly, wet sites in upper foothills and montane zones; southern Interior B.C.

Western Hemlock

Tsuga heterophylla

Height: up to 50 m, with drooping leader
Needles: 1–2 cm long, unequal length; in flat, feathery arrangement
Seed cones: 1–3 cm long, elliptic; hang on short stalks

Western hemlock's hard, strong, even-grained wood is widely used to make cabinets, mouldings and floors, and provides lumber, pilings, poles and pulp. The crushed needles were thought to smell like poison-hemlock plants, hence the common name. The needles are flat, blunt, unequal, and in 2 opposite rows. • In subalpine zones, mountain hemlock (*T. mertensiana*) has cones that are 3–7 cm long and needles in a bottlebrush-like arrangement (not in 2 rows). **Where found:** moist sites from sea level to montane zones; coastal, and Interior wet belt.

Douglas-fir

Pseudotsuga menziesii

Height: up to 70 m
Needles: 2–3 cm long; flat, flexible, often pointed
Seed cones: 5–9 cm long, narrow; yellowish-brown or purplish-brown

This common evergreen with its compact, pyramidal crowns and (often) drooping branches is one of the world's best-known timber-producers. Thick, fire-resistant bark allows some Douglas-firs to live for well over 1000 years and grow to heights of 100 m. Two varieties are native to B.C.: a coastal form, called Douglas-fir, and an Interior form, called Rocky Mountain Douglas-fir. • Douglas-fir is easily identified by its cones, which have promi-nent, 3-pronged bracts that extend beyond the scales. The bracts look like the tails and hind legs of little mice hiding in the cones.
• **Where found:** moist to very dry sites; low to mid-eleva-tion; southern 1/2 of B.C.

Western Yew

Taxus brevifolia

Height: up to 15 m
Needles: 1.5–2 cm long; flat needles, flat sprays arranged in 2 rows
Fruits: bright red, fleshy, berry-like cup, 5–6 mm wide on female plants

This tree's dark, flat evergreen needles and bright, scarlet "berries" make it an attractive ornamental. Male and female cones are on separate plants, and only the female plants have the bright red, poison-ous "berries." • The bark contains taxol, a drug used to treat ovarian and breast cancer. Har-vesting for taxol has ceased in B.C. owing to concerns over the ecological impacts and with research into alternate sources.
• The heavy, fine-grained wood is prized by carvers for its purplish red, papery bark over rose-coloured inner bark. **Where found:** moist, shady sites in zones from low elevation to montane; coastal and southern Interior B.C.

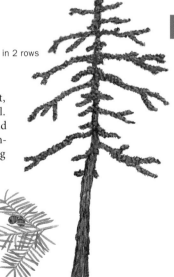

Western Redcedar

Thuja plicata

Height: up to 60 m
Needles: 1–2 mm long, flat, overlapping scales
Seed cones: about 1 cm; 8–12 scales

Known as "trees of life," cedars were the most important and widely used plants for western First Nations. Redcedar provided medicine and materials for Native people throughout their lives. Bark was pounded until fluffy and used for diapers and mattresses. The long, fibrous inner bark strips were woven into baskets, blankets, clothing and ropes. The beautiful, aromatic, reddish wood deters insects and resists decay, making it ideal for carving into dug-out canoes, storage chests and totem poles. Today, redcedar is B.C.'s provincial tree. Wood is widely used for siding, roofing, paneling, doors, patio furniture, chests and caskets. **Where found:** rich, moist to wet, sea level to montane elevations; characteristic tree of the B.C. coast and wetter Interior regions.

Yellow-cedar

Chamaecyparis nootkatensis

Height: up to 40 m
Needles: up to 3 mm long, scale-like, flattened with pointed tips
Seed cones: 8–10 mm long, brownish, woody with triangular scales

Yellow-cedars commonly live 1000–1500 years. The oldest specimen recorded in B.C. to date is 1835 years old, though some individuals almost certainly live more than 2 millennia. These sometimes slow-growing trees may require over 200 years to reach a marketable size. The tough, straight-grained wood was used by nearly every Northwest Coast First Nation for construction and tool-making, ideal for making bows, canoe paddles, boat ribs, ceremonial masks, headdresses, totem poles, chests and fishnet hoops. **Where found:** cool wet forests at sea level (in bogs), and montane to subalpine on moist sites; in coastal B.C. and a few spots in southeastern B.C.

Rocky Mountain Juniper

Juniperus scopulorum

Height: 25–90 m
Needles: 1 cm long; flat, overlapping scales, needle-like when young
Seed cones: blue, berry-like, 5–6 mm across

These small, drought-resistant conifers typically live for 300 years; some may survive up to 1500 years. • Many animals and birds use juniper for cover and food. Bighorn sheep and Townsend's solitaire eat the "berries," helping to disperse the seeds. • Juniper berries are used as a flavouring for gin, beer and other alcoholic drinks. • Seaside juniper *(J. maritima)*, which occur in drier portions of B.C.'s south coast, used to be included in Rocky Mountain juniper but are not actually closely related. **Where found:** dry areas; rocky ridges, open foothills and bluffs, steppe and montane; southern ½ of Interior B.C., rare northwards.

Arbutus

Arbutus menziesii

Height: up to 30 m
Leaves: to 15 cm long; oval, leathery, evergreen
Flowers: 0.6–0.7 cm, greenish white, in drooping clusters, fragrant
Fruit: 1 cm wide, orange-red berries

Arbutus is the only broadleaved evergreen tree native to Canada. • These drought-tolerant trees have distinctive reddish-brown, peeling bark. The tannins in the bark were used as a preservative on wood and ropes, to tan paddles and fish hooks, and as a source of brown dye. • The Latin *Arbutus* and Spanish *madrone* translate to "strawberry tree," referring to the red fruits. **Where found:** dry, sunny, often rocky sites; low elevations; dry climates on southern Pacific coast. **Also known as:** Pacific madrone.

Black Cottonwood

Populus balsamifera ssp. *trichocarpa*

Height: up to 50 m
Leaves: 5–15 cm long; rounded, triangular shape; whitish beneath
Flowers: male (pollen) catkins 2–5 cm long;
female catkins 8–20 cm long
Fruit: capsules, 3–4 mm long, in 12–15 cm long,
hanging, downy catkins

Cottonwoods grow on floodplains or shorelines because the seeds require wet mud to germinate. The trees "snow" (release their "parachute" seeds) in late May or early June, as rivers swollen from spring run-off begin to recede. These fast-growing trees can reach massive proportion. Young trees can grow more than 3.5 m a year, and even big ones can add 1.5 m annually. • Black cottonwood stabilize riverbanks and enhance fish habitat—rotting leaves provide nutrients for insects, which in turn provide food for young salmon and trout. • Balsam poplar *(P. balsamifera* ssp. *balsamifera)*, common in northern B.C., is similar, with leaves that are often greenish or brownish beneath. **Where found:** moist to wet sites, often on shores, low to mid-elevations; southern ⅔ of B.C.

Trembling Aspen

Populus tremuloides

Height: to 25 m
Leaves: 2–8 cm; finely toothed
Flowers: tiny; in slender, hanging catkins (pollen catkins 2–3 cm long, female catkins 4–10 cm long)
Fruit: numerous hairless capsules, in hanging, downy catkins 10 cm long

Suckers from the shallow, spreading roots of this deciduous tree can colonize many hectares of land. Single trunks are relatively short lived, but a colony (clone) can survive for thousands of years. Aspen are gorgeous in autumn, when bright yellow foliage contrasts with silvery bark. • The greenish, photosynthetic bark produces a white powder to protect the trees from ultraviolet radiation in open areas. This powder can be used as sunscreen. **Where found:** dry to moist sites; throughout Interior B.C., rare on the south coast. **Also known as:** quaking aspen, aspen poplar.

Paper Birch

Betula papyrifera

Height: up to 25 m
Leaves: 5–10 cm long; coarsely toothed;
5–9 straight veins per side
Flowers: tiny; male and female flowers
in separate catkins, 2–4 cm long
Fruit: tiny; flat, 2-winged nutlets

This small, showy tree, with its peeling, creamy white bark, occurs across North America. Native peoples used the tree for birch-bark canoes, baskets and message paper. To shield against snow blindness, they made "sunglasses" using bark strips with lenticels. • This pioneer species thrives in full sun and nutrient-rich habitats. In burned or cut areas, it can form near monocultures. • Birch bark is a winter staple for moose and white-tailed deer. Porcupines and snowshoe hares browse on the leaves, seedlings and bark, and common redpolls eat the catkins. • Water birch *(B. occidentalis)* has dark purplish-brown, non-peeling bark and grows in moist, riparian areas of southern Interior B.C., rare northwards. **Where found:** open, often disturbed sites, forest edges on a variety of substrates; throughout, except on coast.

Red Alder

Alnus rubra

Height: up to 25 m
Leaves: 7–13 cm long, broadly elliptical
Flowers: male (pollen) catkins 10–15 cm long;
female catkins in clusters of 3–5
Fruit: brownish cones, 2 cm long

This tree gets its name from the red colour that develops when the bark is scraped or bruised. • Red alder wood was an important fuel for smoking fish, especially salmon. The attractive wood is popular for artistic carvings and bowls. The twigs and inner bark produce a red dye that was used to colour hides and birch-bark baskets. • The bark was used for a variety of medicinal purposes—reputed to have antibiotic properties, it was used as a tonic and an antibacterial wash. The ancient Romans treated tumors with alder leaves, which modern scientists have since learned contain the tumor-suppressing compounds betulin and lupeol. **Where found:** low-elevation moist woods, streambanks, floodplains, cleared land; coastal B.C.

Garry Oak

Quercus garryana

Height: up to 20 m
Leaves: 7–10 cm long; 5–7 deep lobes
Flowers: tiny, inconspicuous catkins (male) and flower clusters (female)
Fruit: edible acorns, 2–3 cm long

The Garry oak savannah is one of Canada's most endangered ecosystems, with an estimated 1% of its original range remaining. Garry oak is the signature plant of this ecosystem, intermixed with a beautiful parkland carpet of spring wildflowers including yellow buttercups, brown chocolate lilies and purple shooting stars. The Garry oak savannah is a cultural artifact, the result of an estimated 5000 years of controlled burning, digging, weeding and other practices by local First Nations peoples to enhance the productivity of edible bulbs and roots as well as acorns and berries. Today, introduced species and habitat loss threaten the ecosystem. **Where found:** dry, rocky slopes or bluffs at low elevations; extreme southwest B.C.

Pacific Dogwood

Cornus nuttallii

Height: up to 20 m
Leaves: 4–10 cm long; oval, deeply veined
Flowers: tiny, white to greenish, often purple-tinged, surrounded by 4–6 showy white bracts
Fruit: red berries, 1 cm across, in clusters

This beautiful, small understorey tree has delicate flowers, shiny red berries and red autumn leaves. The showy, whitish dogwood "flowers" are actually floral bracts that surround the true cluster of tiny, greenish flowers. • Golf-club heads, daggers and engraver's blocks have been made from the tough wood. The berries attract birds and provide food for small mammals. • Pacific dogwood is B.C.'s provincial flower. Unfortunately, many Pacific dogwoods have been lost to dogwood anthracnose (*Discula destructiva*), a fungal disease. **Where found:** moist, well-drained sites, such as along streambeds, in low-elevation mixed forests in southwestern B.C. **Also known as:** western flowering dogwood.

Bigleaf Maple

Acer macrophyllum

Height: up to 35 m
Leaves: 15–30 cm across, 5-lobed
Flowers: 0.3 cm across, greenish yellow, numerous, in hanging clusters
Fruit: paired samaras, 3–6 cm long, wings in a "V" shape

Moss thrives on the bigleaf maple with such exuberance that the bark is often completely enrobed. The moss forms a thick layer in the tree's canopy, creating a "floating soil" onto which other plants sprout and root. • Though the sap of bigleaf maple has lower sugar concentrations than the eastern sugar maple, a small bigleaf maple syrup industry is developing in B.C., producing delicious and distinctively flavoured maple syrup. **Where found:** dry to moist sites; often on sites disturbed by fire, clearing or logging; low to mid-elevations; southern coast.

Douglas Maple

Acer glabrum

Height: to 10 m
Leaves: 7–14 cm long; broad, 3- to 5-lobed, coarse toothed
Flowers: 5 mm across; pale yellowish green, in dense erect clusters
Fruit: samaras, 2 cm long, wings in a "V" shape

This small maple is our most northerly ranging species, found throughout much of the province. It is identified in summer by opposite leaves with 3 prominent lobes (sometimes 2 lower lobes) and small scarlet to pinkish brown keys (samaras), spreading at a 45-degree angle or less. • Douglas maple has no commercial value, but the branches spread toward the ground, take root and grow into dense thickets, controlling erosion on steep banks and ravines. • Vine maple (*A. circinatum*) is a large shrub or tree that grows to 8 m tall, with 7- to 9-lobed leaves, in open forest or streamside in southwestern B.C. **Where found:** moist, mixed woods, thickets; southern ¾ of B.C.

Pacific Crab Apple

Malus fusca

Height: 2–12 m
Leaves: up to 10 cm long, lance-shaped, toothed, often irregularly lobed
Flowers: 2 cm across, white to pink, showy, in flat-topped clusters, fragrant
Fruit: 1–2 cm long oval apples, yellow or reddish at maturity

Pacific crab apples served as an essential food item traditionally, and are also an important food today. Traditionally, large quantities were harvested and either eaten fresh with eulachon oil or stored for the winter. Boxes of Pacific crab apples were a common trade item in the past and were also used as gifts at events such as weddings. The fruit of Pacific crab apple is rich in pectin so it can be added to low-pectin fruits when making jams and jellies. **Where found:** moist woods, swamps, riparian edges, near estuaries; low elevations; coastal B.C.

SHRUBS

The difference between a tree and a shrub is sometimes rather sketchy, but in general, shrubs are small woody plants less than 6 metres tall. They are typically bushy owing to multiple small trunks and branches that emerge from near the ground, and many species produce soft berries. Some shrubs occur in open, sunny areas, and others are important dominant components of the understorey in forests. They provide habitat and shelter for a variety of animals, and their berries, leaves and often bark are crucial sources of food. The tasty berries of some shrubs have been a staple of Native and traditional foods, and they are still enjoyed by people throughout British Columbia.

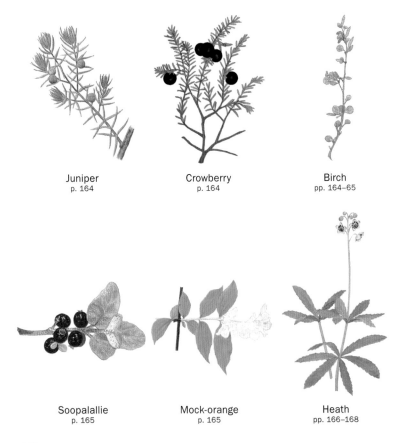

Juniper
p. 164

Crowberry
p. 164

Birch
pp. 164–65

Soopalallie
p. 165

Mock-orange
p. 165

Heath
pp. 166–168

Falsebox
p. 169

Oregon-grape
p. 169

Willow
p. 169

Dogwood
p. 170

Devil's Club
p. 170

Rose
pp. 170–74

Scotch Broom
p. 174

Aster
p. 174

Buckthorn
p. 175

Gooseberry
p. 175

Honeysuckle
pp. 176–77

Poison-ivy
p. 177

Common Juniper

Juniperus communis

Height: prostrate, trailing, usually less than 1 m tall and 2.5 m wide
Needles: 5–12 mm long, narrow, lance-shaped
Seed cones: female 6–10 mm across, bluish, berry-like; male catkin-like cones

Common juniper grows over much of the world and is most famous as the flavouring for gin. The blue-grey "berries" of this shrub are, in fact, tiny cones with 3–8 fleshy scales. The strongly flavoured berries are occasionally added to wild game dishes but are generally considered distasteful. Pregnant women or people with kidney problems should not eat juniper. • Creeping juniper (*J. horizontalis*), also widespread in our region, is a low, creeping evergreen shrub (up to 25 cm tall), with overlapping, scale-like leaves. **Where found:** dry, open sites, coastal bogs; throughout.

Crowberry

Empetrum nigrum

Height: creeping evergreen, to 30 cm long
Leaves: 3–8 mm, needle-like
Flowers: tiny, purplish crimson
Fruit: berry-like drupes, 4–6 mm

This creeping, evergreen shrub forms dense mats on the forest floor. It is commonly found in muskeg, cool, spruce forests and on tundra. • The black, edible berries may be harvested in autumn or the following spring. Haida and Tsimshian peoples ate small quantities of the berries fresh or mixed them with grease, but they were a more popular food with Arctic aboriginal groups. The berries can also be made into jams and jellies or added to baked goods. Bears eat large amounts of crowberries. **Where found:** coniferous forest floor, acidic peatlands and alpine heaths; throughout B.C. from low elevations to alpine.

Scrub Birch

Betula nana

Height: up to 2 m
Leaves: 1–2 cm long, round, coarsely toothed, leathery
Flowers: pollen catkins 1–2 cm long, hanging; seed catkins 1 cm long, erect
Fruit: 2 mm wide, round winged nutlets

Scrub birch is a common shrub of the Interior mountains and alpine. Young branches are covered with tiny, crystalline resin glands. • Some Native peoples chewed the stems then packed the poultice into deep cuts to stop bleeding. Boiling the leaves and branches into tea was said to aid in weight loss, and tea made from the cones was used to relieve menstrual cramps. **Where found:** moist to wet, open sites such as bogs, fens, marshes and rocky slopes; montane to alpine in B.C.'s Interior. **Also known as:** bog birch, *B. glandulosum*.

Beaked Hazelnut

Corylus cornuta

Height: up to 3 m
Leaves: 5–10 cm long, elliptical, heart-shaped or round base
Flowers: in catkins; male hanging, 4–7 cm; female tiny, crimson
Fruit: spherical nuts, 1–1.5 cm long

Plentiful, edible wild hazelnuts are rich in protein but sometimes become infested with grubs just when they are ready to harvest. A bristly, greenish, beaked husk surrounds each round nut. Nuts are usually in groups of 2 or 3. They can be roasted and eaten whole or ground into flour. • If you have sharp eyes, you may spot the hazelnut's tiny, crimson female flowers in spring. • The town of Hazelton was named after this plant. **Where found:** moist, well-drained woodlands; forested areas of Interior south of 57° N, and on southern Vancouver Is. and Fraser Valley.

Soopolallie

Shepherdia canadensis

Height: 1–2 m
Leaves: 2–6 cm long, elliptical, greenish above, silvery below
Flowers: 4 mm wide, greenish yellow; male and female flowers on separate plants
Fruit: bright red, oval berry, 6–8 mm

This deciduous shrub has dark green leaves that are silvery below with star-shaped hairs and rust-coloured scales. The juicy, translucent red berries are quite sour, but many Native peoples enjoyed them. • Soopolallie contains a bitter, soapy substance (saponin) that foams when beaten. They were whipped like egg whites to make a foamy "ice-cream" dessert, which was sweetened with other berries and, later, with sugar. **Where found:** open woods, streambanks; throughout forested areas, except absent from Haida Gwaii and northern Vancouver Is. **Also known as:** Canada buffaloberry, soapberry.

Mock-orange

Philadelphus lewisii

Height: to 3 m
Leaves: 3–5 cm long, oval, 3 major veins
Flowers: 2–3 cm wide, white, fragrant, usually 4-petals, in clusters of 3–15
Fruit: 4-chambered capsule, 1 cm wide

This attractive shrub, with its dark green foliage and showy flowers, makes a lovely addition to sunny or partly shaded gardens, and several cultivars are available from greenhouses. • Mock-orange wood is stiff and hard and was traditionally used to make such items as knitting needles, birch-bark basket rims, pipe stems, fish spears and snowshoes. The plant was also used as soap, either through soaking the bark, mashing the leaves in water, or bruising the leaves and flowers with the hands to produce lather. **Where found:** open forests, forest areas, brushy areas, dry slopes; southern B.C.

Prince's Pine

Chimaphila umbellata

Height: 10–30 cm
Leaves: 2–8 cm long, elliptical, toothed, leathery
Flowers: less than 1 cm across, pinkish, bell-shaped
Fruit: rounded capsules, 5–7 mm across

The leaves of this semi-woody, evergreen shrub are dark, glossy green above and pale beneath. The flowers are waxy, and the fruits are round capsules. This attractive plant needs certain soil fungi to live and often dies when transplanted, so it is best enjoyed in the wild. • Prince's pine has been used to flavour candy, soft drinks (especially root beer) and traditional beers. Several Native groups smoked the dried leaves. **Where found:** mesic to dry wooded, usually coniferous sites, throughout B.C. **Also known as:** pipsissewa.

Kinnikinnick

Arctostaphylos uva-ursi

Height: to 10 cm
Leaves: 1–3 cm long, dark green, oval, leathery
Flowers: 4–6 mm long, pinkish, urn-shaped
Fruit: dull red berry-like drupes, 6–10 mm

Thick, leathery evergreen leaves help this common, mat-forming shrub survive on dry, sunny slopes where others would perish. The flowers nod in small clusters, and trailing branches, which may be up to a metre long, send down roots. • The red "berries" are edible but are rather mealy and tasteless. To reduce their dryness, they were traditionally cooked and mixed with grease or fish eggs. • The glossy leaves were widely used for smoking, both alone and later with tobacco. **Where found:** sandy, well-drained, open or wooded sites; throughout. **Also known as:** bearberry.

Pink Mountain-heather

Phyllodoce empetriformis

Height: up to 40 cm
Leaves: 0.5–1.2 cm long, needle-like, grooved
Flowers: 5–8 mm long, pink, bell-shaped
Fruit: 3–4 mm wide, round capsules

These bright, rose-pink clusters of tiny bells on deep green mats delight hikers across alpine slopes. Needle-like leaves help these ground-hugging plants to survive in areas where frozen soil and cold, dry winds limit water. The fruits are erect, round capsules and the young shrub is glandular-hairy. • Mountain-heather could be mistaken for crowberry, but crowberry has shorter leaves, inconspicuous flowers and juicy black berries (rather than dry capsules). **Where found:** dry to moist slopes in subalpine and alpine zones; throughout (except northeast B.C. and Haida Gwaii).

Salal

Gaultheria shallon

Height: up to 5 m
Leaves: 5–10 cm long, oval, leathery, glossy
Flowers: to 1 cm long, urn-shaped, white to pinkish, in clusters
Fruit: bluish-black edible berry, 6–10 mm across

The edible berries of salal were an important food source to
Native peoples, but they are mealy and were typically dried or
mixed with animal fat or fish oil or eggs. A tea made from the
leaves was used to treat several ailments, or the leaves were
dried along with kinnikinnick leaves and smoked like tobacco.
Where found: dry to wet, conifer forests and bogs from sea level
to montane zones; coast (rare in southeast B.C.).

Oval-leaved Blueberry

Vaccinium ovalifolium

Height: up to 2 m
Leaves: 1–4 cm long, oval
Flowers: 3–5 mm long, bell-shaped, pinkish
Fruit: blue berries, 6–9 mm across

Plentiful blueberries were the most important fruits for
coastal and Interior Native peoples, and blueberry picking
remains a favourite family tradition today. Traditionally the
berries were eaten fresh, dried or preserved in grease. The roots and
stems were boiled into various medicinal teas. • Today, we enjoy blueberry pie, jam, pancakes and even blueberry wine, and blueberries are
widely cultivated. • Sixteen species of *Vaccinium* grow in B.C., including blueberries
and both red and black huckleberries. **Where found:** forests and clearings at low to
subalpine elevations; throughout central and southern B.C.

False Azalea

Menziesia ferruginea

Height: up to 2 m
Leaves: 3–5 cm long, in clusters along branches
Flowers: 6–8 mm long, salmon to yellowish, urn-shaped
Fruit: oval capsules, 5–7 mm long

This deciduous shrub is sometimes called "fool's huckleberry," because it looks like a huckleberry, but its fruit is a dry
capsule, not a berry. • Like many members of the heath family
(Ericaceae), this plant contains the poison andromedotoxin. • The
sticky-hairy twigs of false azalea smell skunky when crushed. The
thin, dull, pale green, glandular-hairy leaves turn crimson in
autumn and are mostly clustered near branch tips. **Where found:**
dry to wet woods in low to subalpine zones; throughout.

Labrador Tea

Ledum groenlandicum

Height: to 1.5 m
Leaves: 1–5 cm long, oblong, leathery, rusty below
Flowers: 8–10 mm wide, white, in umbrella-shaped clusters
Fruit: dry, drooping capsules, 5–7 mm

This evergreen shrub saves energy by keeping its leaves year-round. The leaves have a thick, leathery texture, rolled edges and distinctive rusty-coloured, woolly hairs on their undersides, all adaptations that help the plant conserve moisture. Labrador tea may also produce chemicals that discourage other plants from growing nearby. • First Nations peoples and early settlers made the leaves and flowers into a tea that was rich in vitamin C. **Caution:** Consuming large amounts can be toxic; do not confuse this plant with other poisonous heaths such as bog laurel *(Kalmia polifolia)* or bog rosemary. **Where found:** moist, acidic, nutrient-poor soils, often (in the northern Interior) associated with black spruce; throughout except grasslands.

Bog Rosemary

Andromeda polifolia

Height: to 80 cm
Leaves: 1–5 cm long, dull green, leathery, oblong
Flowers: 6 mm long, white-pinkish, urn-shaped
Fruit: small, round capsules, 6 mm wide

Despite resembling and sharing the name of a common kitchen herb, bog rosemary contains poisonous andromedotoxin compounds that can cause breathing problems, vomiting and even death if ingested. • The leathery leaves of this plant curl under, and their undersides are covered with fine hairs to help prevent moisture loss. • Bog rosemary has rounded stems and bluish green, alternate leaves, unlike bog laurel *(Kalmia polifolia)*, which has flattened stems and shiny, green, opposite leaves. **Where found:** wet areas, coniferous swamps, sphagnum bogs, lakeshores; throughout, except grasslands.

White Rhododendron

Rhododendron albiflorum

Height: 1–2.5 m
Leaves: 4–9 cm long, evergreen, leathery
Flowers: white, bell-shaped, 1–2 cm wide, in clusters in leaf axils
Fruit: woody capsules, 6–8 mm long

In spring, mountainsides blush with white blooms, and the understories of coniferous forests are brightened with this colourful species. It often grows with false azalea and copperbrush *(Cladothamnus pyroliforus)*. • Rhododendrons are poisonous plants, containing a neurotoxin called grayanotoxin. Though wild animals are wary, livestock is often careless, and this plant has to be cleared from grazing lands. • Pacific rhododendron *(R. macrophyllum)* has pink flowers and is found in southwestern B.C. **Where found:** wet to fairly dry coniferous or mixed forests; throughout most of B.C., but absent in the far north. **Also known as:** white-flowered rhododendron.

Falsebox

Paxistima myrsinites

Height: 20–80 cm
Leaves: 1–3 cm long, leathery, shiny
Flowers: 3–4 mm wide, maroon, in small clusters
Fruit: tiny oval capsules

The glossy, stiff, leathery leaves of these low, branched, evergreen shrubs blanket the floor of many mountain forests.
Sprays of falsebox are often used in flower arrangements, and
over-collecting has depleted many populations. • The greenish
brown to dark reddish flowers are borne in small clusters in the
leaf axils. • To remember this plant's unusual scientific name, just repeat "pa
kissed ma." **Where found:** mesic forests to well-drained, open sites in lowland,
foothills and montane zones; central and southern B.C. **Also known as:** mountain
boxwood, *Pachistima myrsinites*.

Tall Oregon-Grape

Berberis aquifolium

Height: up to 3 m
Leaves: 5–11 holly-like leaflets, 4–7 cm long on central stalk
Flower: tiny yellow flowers in a 2–5 cm inflorescence
Fruit: blue grape-like berries, to 1.4 cm diameter

These evergreens are popular in gardens with red, purple and green
spiny winter leaves making them attractive Christmas decorations similar to
holly. The juicy grape-like berries are sour, but can be eaten raw, make good jam
and wine and are sometimes mixed with salal to make jelly. Berry production can
vary greatly from year to year, and the fruits are sometimes rendered inedible by grub
infestations. • Boiled, shredded root bark produces a brilliant yellow dye. **Where found:**
exposed areas, dry rocky sites on lowland to montane slopes; southern B.C.

Pussy Willow

Salix discolor

Height: to 6 m
Leaves: 3–10 cm long, somewhat variable, elliptical, sometimes
wavy-edged
Flowers: tiny, on hairy catkins 2–4 cm long
Fruit: hairy capsules, 8–10 mm long

B.C. has nearly 50 species of willow, and many are tough to identify. With its hairy felt-like catkins, pussy willow is common and distinctive. •
Growing quickly with extensive root systems, willows are good for erosion control and re-vegetating burned areas. • The stems of some species are used for
wickerwork or, traditionally, for dream-catcher charms. The wet inner bark fibres
were twisted into fishing nets and ropes. The hollow stems were used as drinking
straws or for making pipes. Green branches can be used to smoke meat. • Many
butterfly species, including the mourning cloak, use willow as the larval host
plant. **Where found:** moist to wet open sites; throughout.

Red-osier Dogwood

Cornus sericea

Height: to 5 m
Leaves: 2–10 cm long, egg- or lance-shaped
Flowers: 5 mm across, white, in dense flat-topped clusters
Fruit: white berry-like drupes, 7–9 mm across

This attractive, hardy, deciduous shrub has distinctive purple to red branches with white flowers in spring, red leaves in autumn and white, berry-like drupes in winter. The opposite leaves have 5–7 prominent veins. Dogwood is easily grown from cuttings and makes an interesting addition to a native plant garden.
• Native peoples smoked the dried inner bark alone or mixed it with tobacco or common bearberry leaves. The flexible branches can be woven into baskets. **Where found:** moist to wet, usually open sites; throughout. **Also known as:** *Cornus stolonifera.*

Devil's Club

Oplopanax horridus

Height: 1–3 m, armed with yellow spines
Leaves: large, to 35 cm wide, maple-leaf shaped, spiny undersides
Flowers: small, whitish, in compact pyramidal head
Fruit: bright red, shiny berries in showy pyramidal cluster

Devil's club is closely related to ginseng and is one of B.C.'s most powerful and important medicinal plants. The root tea has been reported to stimulate the respiratory tract and to help bring up phlegm when treating colds, bronchitis and pneumonia. It has also been used to treat diabetes, because it helps to regulate blood sugar levels and to reduce the craving for sugar. The spines of devil's club break off easily and cause allergic reaction in some people. **Where found:** moist to wet, shady lowland to subalpine sites; all but northeast B.C.

Chokecherry

Prunus virginiana

Height: up to 6 m
Leaves: 3–10 cm long, toothed, broadly oval with sharp tip
Flowers: tiny, white cup-shaped flowers hang in long cylindrical clusters
Fruit: reddish to blackish cherries, 8–12 mm across

Chokecherry has long, bottlebrush-like clusters of flowers and hanging clusters of shiny, crimson fruit that turn black with age. The sour cherry flesh can be eaten raw or preserved, but the stones, bark, wood and leaves contain toxic hydrocyanic acid.
• Many species of moths and butterflies use chokecherry as a host plant. • Bitter cherry *(P. emarginata)* and pin cherry *(P. pensylvanica)* have flat-topped flower clusters. Bitter cherry has red to black cherries 8–12 mm long and grows mainly in coastal areas; pin cherry has smaller red cherries 4–8 mm long and is found in the Interior. **Where found:** open sites, fencerows, streams, forest edges; throughout.

Saskatoon

Amelanchier alnifolia

Height: up to 6 m
Leaves: 2–5 cm long; oval to round
Flowers: about 1 cm across; white, showy, 5-petals, in clusters
Fruit: dark purple berry-like pomes, 5–10 mm wide

These hardy, deciduous shrubs or small trees have beautiful white blossoms in spring, delicious fruit in summer and scarlet leaves in autumn. • The sweet, juicy "berries" of this shrub were an important food source for many Native peoples. Large quantities were dried and mixed with meat and fat, or added to stews. Today, saskatoons are used in baked goods, jams, jellies, syrups and wine. Many mammals and birds also feast on the berries, including black bears, snowshoe hares, flying squirrels, pheasants, grouse, woodpeckers and songbirds. **Where found:** dry, often sandy woods, rocky sites, forest edges; throughout.

Black Hawthorn

Crataegus douglasii

Height: up to 8 m
Leaves: 3–6 cm long; leathery, oval, with 5–9 lobes at top end
Flowers: 1 cm across, white, in clusters
Fruit: blackish-purple haws (pomes), about 1 cm long

This easily recognized, widespread species has thorns 1–2 cm long and branched clusters of white, unpleasant-smelling flowers. The purplish-black haws resemble tiny apples and remain on the plant throughout winter. The haws of all species are edible but usually seedy or mealy. • Hawthorn thickets provide shelter and food for many small animals that, in turn, help distribute the fruit. • Red hawthorn *(C. columbiana)*, also found in southern B.C., grows to 4 m tall, has longer thorns (>3 cm long) and red haws. **Where found:** forest edges, thickets, riparian areas; lowland to montane; southern B.C.

Western Mountain-ash

Sorbus scopulina

Height: 1–4 m
Leaves: pinnately divided into 9–13 opposite leaflets, each 3–6 cm long
Flowers: tiny, white, in dense 9–15 cm wide clusters
Fruit: shiny, red-orange berry-like pomes, 7–8 mm across

This extremely showy shrub has sharp-tipped leaves and bright clusters of white flowers or glossy clusters of reddish berries. The juicy berries attract many birds such as cedar waxwings, and the more northerly bohemian waxwing's range seems largely tied to mountain-ash. The decorative berries last well and are sometimes made into jams and jellies. • Sitka mountain-ash *(S. sitchensis)* has bluish-green, round-tipped leaves and also grows on foothills and mountain slopes. **Where found:** moist, open or shaded sites, foothills to subalpine; throughout.

Trailing Blackberry

Rubus ursinus

Height: trailing, to 5 m long, up to 50 cm
Leaves: 3 leaflets, 3–7 cm long; toothed
Flowers: to 4 cm across; white to pink, in clusters
Fruit: black berries, to 1 cm long

Blackberries, and raspberries and relatives [salmonberries (*R. spectabilis*), thimbleberries (*R. parviflorus*) and cloudberries (*R. chamaemorus*)], are all closely related members of the genus *Rubus*. The best way to separate them is by their fruits: blackberries have a solid "core," and raspberries and relatives have a hollow core. • Abundant, edible blackberries may be enjoyed fresh or preserved. Our native species, the deciduous trailing blackberry, has 3 leaflets. The most common introduced species is the evergreen Himalayan blackberry (*R. armeniacus*), an upright shrub that grows 4 m tall with 5 leaflets. **Where found:** thickets and open, disturbed sites; low to mid-elevations; southwestern B.C.

Wild Red Raspberry

Rubus idaeus

Height: 1–2 m
Leaves: 4–20 cm long; compound, with 3–5 toothed leaflets
Flowers: 8–12 mm wide; white, 5 petals
Fruit: red raspberries (drupelets), 1 cm across

Delicious, plump raspberries can be eaten straight off the bush or made into jams, jellies or pies. Tender young shoots may be eaten raw once the prickly outer layer has been peeled off. Fresh or completely dried leaves make excellent tea, but wilted leaves can be toxic. • Traditionally, raspberry-leaf tea was given to women to treat painful menstruation or during childbirth to reduce labour pains, increase milk flow or aid in recovery. **Where found:** thickets, clearings, open woods; throughout the Interior, uncommon on the coast.

Prickly Wild Rose

Rosa acicularis

Height: 20–120 cm
Leaves: compound, 3–9 oblong leaflets, each 2–5 cm long
Flowers: 5–7 cm across; showy, pink
Fruit: red hips, about 15 mm long

These sweet-smelling deciduous shrubs, with their fragrant pink rose flowers and scarlet, berry-like hips are widespread across B.C. Interior. The stems are covered with many small bristles. • Most parts of rose shrubs are edible, and the sweet hips are rich in vitamin C. Avoid the seeds; their sliver-like hairs can irritate the digestive tract. • Wood rose (*R. woodsii*) has fewer, more scattered thorns, usually in pairs at stem nodes, and is also common and widespread in Interior B.C. **Where found:** dry to moist sites; throughout B.C. Interior, uncommon on the coast.

Ninebark

Physocarpus capitatus

Height: up to 4 m
Leaves: 3–8 cm long, 3- or 5-lobed
Flowers: 1 cm wide, white, 5 petals, in rounded clusters
Fruit: reddish brown follicles, 1 cm long, in dense, upright clusters

Although it is slightly toxic, many Native groups used this plant medicinally, following the old adage that "what doesn't kill you, cures you." • This shrub is named for the supposedly 9 layers of bark that can be peeled away from the stem. • The leaves turn to intense reds and oranges in fall. **Where found:** wet, somewhat open places such as in thickets along streams and lakes, coastal marshes and edges of moist woodlands; low to mid-elevations in southwestern and southeastern B.C.

Oceanspray

Holodiscus discolor

Height: up to 4 m
Leaves: 3–6 cm long, coarsely toothed or lobed, hairy
Flowers: tiny, creamy white, in upright to hanging clusters 10–17 cm long
Fruit: tiny, light brown, in large clusters that persist through winter

As its name attests, oceanspray is very tolerant of salt spray and maritime conditions. Its hardiness makes it a pioneer species on disturbed sites. • The wood is extremely hard—other common names included "arrow-wood" and "ironwood"—and straight young shoots were used to make arrow, spear and harpoon shafts. It could be made harder by heating over a fire and polishing with horsetail stems. • The small, dry, flattened fruits of this species can be eaten raw or cooked. **Where found:** coast to low montane forest edges and cliffsides in southern B.C.

Shrubby Cinquefoil

Dasiphora floribunda

Height: up to 1–1.5 m
Leaves: 2 cm long; pinnately compound, 3–7 (usually 5) leaflets
Flowers: 2–3 cm wide; yellow, saucer-shaped, single or in small clusters at branch tips
Fruit: tiny; egg-shaped, hairy achenes

Commonly planted in parking lot islands, shrubby cinquefoil is a common garden ornamental with many cultivars. In the wild, it often indicates high-quality habitats. • Traditionally, the leaves were used to spice meat and were boiled into a tea that was high in calcium. Medicinal teas, made of the leaves, stems and roots, have mild astringent properties and were used to treat congestion, tuberculosis and fevers. **Where found:** wet prairies, fens, rocky shores; throughout, but rare on the coast. **Also known as:** *Potentilla fruticosa* and *Pentaphylloides floribunda*.

Birch-leaved Spirea

Spiraea betulifolia

Height: up to 60 cm
Leaves: 3–6 cm; oval, coarsely double-toothed above middle
Flowers: 5–8 mm; white or purplish, in nearly flat-topped clusters
Fruit: clusters of small pods

These attractive deciduous shrubs are easily overlooked, but when they bloom, their showy flower clusters catch the eyes of passersby. • Birch-leaved spirea is hardy and easily grown from cuttings, shoots or seeds, but once established, it spreads rapidly by rhizomes, and can become difficult to control. • Grouse eat the young leaves, and deer also browse on these shrubs. **Where found:** dry to moist forests; open, rocky slopes; low to subalpine.

Scotch Broom

Cytisus scoparius

Height: up to 3 m
Leaves: 2 cm long, divided into 3 leaflets
Flowers: 2 cm long, yellow
Fruit: flattened, black pods, 2–3 cm long

Although bright masses of golden-yellow Scotch broom flowers fill hedges, ditches and roadsides with radiant colour, this shrub is not regarded with much pleasure by botanists—it's classified as a noxious weed. An invasive, introduced species from Europe, it is amazingly prolific and spreads rapidly over wide areas. Reportedly, just 3 seeds planted on Vancouver Is. in 1850 subsequently colonized the entire island. **Where found:** low elevations; open and disturbed sites; invades natural meadows and open forests; southern B.C.

Big Sagebrush

Artemisia tridentata

Height: to 2 m
Leaves: 1–4 cm long, silvery, 3 teeth at the tip
Flowers: very small, yellow, in heads 7 cm wide
Fruit: granular achenes

Sagebrush leaves and branches, with their pungent aroma and greyish, shredding bark, have been used in a wide variety of medicines and burned as ceremonial smudges. The aromatic, volatile oils have been used in shampoos and as insect repellents. • Big sagebrush is in the sunflower family and is not related to sages in the mint family. • This plant is found in similar habitats as rabbitbrush and similar-looking bitterbrush *(Purshia tridentata)*, which has silvery, 3-toothed, wedge-shaped leaves. **Where found:** often covering many acres of dry plains and slopes; southern Interior B.C. and the East Kootenays.

Rabbitbrush

Ericameria nauseosa

Height: up to 1 m
Leaves: 2–5 cm long, narrow, grey-green, velvety
Flowers: 5 mm wide, yellow, in dense clusters
Fruit: tufted achenes

In late summer, these flat-topped, deciduous shrubs cover dry slopes with splashes of yellow. A hardy species, this plant thrives on poor soils and in harsh conditions. • Native peoples made medicinal teas from the roots or leaves to treat coughs, colds, fevers and menstrual pain. The dense branches were used to cover and carpet sweathouses, and they were burned slowly to smoke hides. Boiled flowerheads produced a lemon-yellow dye for wool, leather and baskets. **Where found:** dry, plains, foothills and montane zones; southern Interior B.C. and the East Kootenays. **Also known as:** *Chrysothamnus nauseosus*.

Cascara

Rhamnus purshiana

Height: 10 m
Leaves: 6–12 cm long, oval, dark, shiny, with conspicuous veins
Flowers: 3–4 mm long, greenish yellow, 5 petals
Fruit: berry, 5–8 mm across, bright red maturing to deep purple or black

Cascara is the largest buckthorn species. • The bark of these shrubs or small trees has been used as a laxative for thousands of years. The dried bark was traditionally used to make medicinal teas, but today it is usually administered as a liquid extract or elixir, or in tablet form. The edible fruit does not have laxative properties but is not very tasty anyway. **Where found:** moist, acidic soils in shady clearings or in the understorey of forest edges; mixed forests; low to mid-elevations; southern B.C., most common in southwest.

Black Gooseberry

Ribes lacustre

Height: to 2 m
Leaves: 3–4 cm wide; maple-like, 3–5 pointed lobes
Flowers: 1.5–2 mm long petals; reddish, saucer-shaped, in clusters of 7–15
Fruit: bristly dark purple berries, 4–8 mm across

There are 16 species of native currants and gooseberries in British Columbia; all are edible, but flavour varies greatly with species, habitat and season. The fruit may be eaten raw, cooked or dried. Mixed with other berries, they are used to flavour liqueurs or make wines. Currants are high in pectin and make excellent jams and jellies. Small mammals and birds also consume currants. • Spines of bristly black currant can cause an allergic reaction in some people. • Wild currants are the intermediate host for blister rust, a virulent disease of native 5-needled pines. **Where found:** moist, wooded or open sites; throughout.

Common Snowberry

Symphoricarpos albus

Height: to 3 m
Leaves: 2–4 cm long, oval
Flowers: 4–7 mm long, pink to white, bell-shaped
Fruit: white, berry-like, 6–10 mm long

The name "snowberry" refers to the waxy, white, berry-like drupes that remain in small clusters near branch tips through winter. **Caution:** All parts of this deciduous shrub are toxic and will cause vomiting and diarrhea. • Some Native groups called the fruits "corpse berries," because they were believed to be the ghosts of saskatoons—part of the spirit world, not to be eaten by the living. • The broadly funnel-shaped flowers have hairy centres. • The closely related western snowberry *(S. occidentalis)* has thicker, oblong leaves and clusters of greenish white berries. **Where found:** well-drained sites; throughout.

Twinflower

Linnaea borealis

Height: 3–10 cm; loose mats, erect branches
Leaves: 1–2 cm long, evergreen, oval
Flowers: on stalks 3–10 cm tall; pairs of pink bells, 1–1.5 cm long, trumpet-like
Fruit: dry nutlets, 2–3 mm

This trailing, semi-woody evergreen is an excellent native ground cover in partially shaded sites. The small, delicate pairs of pink bells are easily overlooked among other plants on the forest floor, but their sweet perfume may draw you to them in the evening. • Hooked bristles on the tiny, egg-shaped nutlets catch on fur, feathers or clothing of passersby, who then carry these inconspicuous hitchhikers to new locations. **Where found:** moist, open or shaded sites; throughout.

Highbush-cranberry

Viburnum edule

Height: up to 3.5 m
Leaves: 5–11 cm long; 3 pointed, spreading lobes
Flowers: 1–2 cm wide; white, in flat-topped clusters
Fruit: orange to red berry-like drupes, 1–1.5 cm

Shiny, red to orange highbush-cranberry fruit makes a tart, tasty trailside snack and is easy to pick for use in jams and jellies. The berry-like fruits remain above the snow in winter. Raw fruits should not be eaten in large quantities because they can cause vomiting and severe cramps. • American bush-cranberry *(V. opulus)* has much more deeply 3-lobed leaves and is a species of southern B.C. **Where found:** moist habitats, wetland margins and streamsides; throughout.

176

Black Twinberry

Lonicera involucrata

Height: to 5 m
Leaves: opposite, 5–15 cm long, lance-shaped
Flowers: in pairs, yellow, tubular, cupped by 1–2 cm long, purplish bracts
Fruit: in pairs, purplish black berries, 8–12 mm across

The unusual, shiny berries of these deciduous shrubs, with their broad, spreading, backward-bending, shiny red to purplish bracts, catch the eyes of passersby and also of hungry bears and birds. **Caution:** Despite their tempting appearance, these berries are unpalatable, and they can be toxic. • Many other honeysuckles occur in our region. Twining honeysuckle *(L. dioica)* has oval leaves and yellow-orange, funnel-shaped flowers. **Where found:** moist to wet, usually shaded sites; throughout B.C.

Elderberry

Sambucus racemosa

Height: to 6 m
Leaves: opposite, compound, 5–7 leaflets each 5–15 cm long
Flowers: tiny (to 5 mm wide), whitish, in clusters
Fruit: red or black, berry-like drupes, 5–6 mm across

Large, showy clusters of elderberry flowers are conspicuous in early summer along country roadsides. Later, attractive panicles of berry-like drupes appear. The berries can be made into jam, jelly, pies and wine, but raw berries are toxic (cooking destroys the toxins). • There are two common and widespread varieties of elderberry in B.C.: black elderberry (var. *melanocarpa*), with black or purplish black fruits, is the common Interior species; and coastal red elderberry (var. *arborescens*), with red fruits, is the common coastal species. **Where found:** moist, sunny sites and forest edges in lowlands to montane, coastal (coastal red elderberry) or mostly Interior (black elderberry).

Western Poison-ivy

Toxicodendron rydbergii

Height: shrub to 2 m
Leaves: 5–15 cm long; compound, 3 leaflets
Flowers: 1–3 mm across; greenish white
Fruit: white to greenish-yellow berries, 5 mm across

Western poison-ivy is rather showy, especially in autumn when leaflets turn red and ripe berries become white. Plants may take the form of trailing ground cover or small, erect shrubs. Many species of birds eat the fruit. A brush with this plant can cause a severe allergic reaction, obvious in an itchy rash and swelling. To hyper-responders, contact can even be life-threatening. The rash can sometimes be alleviated by washing with plenty of soap, but if symptoms worsen, seek medical attention. • **Where found:** dry to mesic upland sites; uncommon in southern Interior B.C., rare on the south coast.

FORBS, FERNS & GRASSES

Forbs include all non-woody, flowering plants that are not grass-like (grasses, sedges, rushes are graminoids). Forbs are often perennials that grow from a persistent rootstock, but many are short-lived annuals. A great variety of plants are forbs, including all our spring wildflowers, several flowering wetland plants, herbs grown for food or medicine and numerous weeds. Many herbs are used for adding flavour to foods and in herbal remedies, aromatherapy and dyes. Culinary herbs are typically made from the leaves of non-woody plants, but medicinal herbs are made from flowers, fruit, seeds, bark or roots of both non-woody and woody plants. Various forbs also flower into unique, delicate and beautiful colours and forms. They are the inspiration of artists and poets and are often symbols of romance, or have meanings attached to them through folklore, legend or superstition. Forbs are also vital to the ecology of the plant communities in which they occur as food sources for pollinating insects and other animals, host plants for moths and butterflies, nest material for birds and cover for many animal species.

The forbs illustrated here are but the most frequent and likely to be seen examples. British Columbia hosts several thousand species of native forbs, far more than we could hope to include. The species we have included should provide a good starting point for those wishing to delve into the spectacular and diverse flora of our region.

| Orchid | Iris | Lily | Dogwood | Arum | Cactus |
| p. 180 | p. 180 | p. 181–84 | p. 184 | p. 185 | p. 185 |

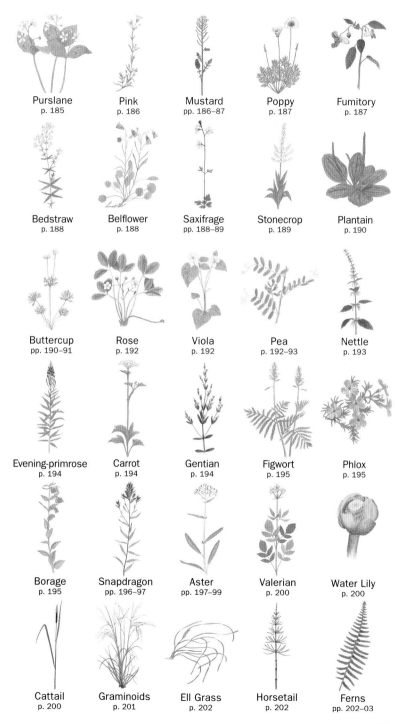

Purslane
p. 185

Pink
p. 186

Mustard
pp. 186–87

Poppy
p. 187

Fumitory
p. 187

Bedstraw
p. 188

Belflower
p. 188

Saxifrage
pp. 188–89

Stonecrop
p. 189

Plantain
p. 190

Buttercup
pp. 190–91

Rose
p. 192

Viola
p. 192

Pea
p. 192–93

Nettle
p. 193

Evening-primrose
p. 194

Carrot
p. 194

Gentian
p. 194

Figwort
p. 195

Phlox
p. 195

Borage
p. 195

Snapdragon
pp. 196–97

Aster
pp. 197–99

Valerian
p. 200

Water Lily
p. 200

Cattail
p. 200

Graminoids
p. 201

Ell Grass
p. 202

Horsetail
p. 202

Ferns
pp. 202–03

Yellow Lady's-slipper

Cypripedium parviflorum

Height: 10–70 cm
Leaves: to 20 cm long; lance-shaped
Flowers: 4 twisted petals around a yellow, 3.5 cm long, sac-like pouch
Fruit: oblong capsules

Finding any of our native orchids is always a treat—more than 30 species are in our region, and none top this stunner. The large, sac-like flowers are adapted for pollination by large bumble bees. The plants depend on special mycorrhzal fungi for nutrient intake, water absorption and seed growth. Do not transplant these unusual orchids—they will likely not survive without the fungi. **Where found:** moist to dry forests, low to subalpine, Interior B.C. and northern Vancouver Is.

Rattlesnake-plantain

Goodyera oblongifolia

Height: 20–40 cm
Leaves: 3–10 cm long; in basal rosette, oblong, often mottled or striped with white
Flowers: dull white to green, on extended terminal spike
Fruit: erect capsules, 1 cm long

Rattlesnake-plantain and various bog orchids (*Habenaria* or *Platanthera* spp.) are some of B.C.'s most common orchids. • The plant's mottled leaves resemble snakeskin (hence the name), and early settlers believed these leaves could be used to treat rattlesnake bites. The basal leaves resemble those of common plantain, thus the second half of the name. • Children used to play with the leaves, rubbing to separate the layers and then inflating the leaves like balloons! **Where found:** moist to dry forests, low to montane, throughout south of 56° N.

Common Blue-eyed Grass

Sisyrinchium montanum

Height: 10–50 cm
Leaves: 1–3.5 mm wide; grass-like
Flowers: 8–10 mm long; blue to violet, 6 pointed tepals, yellow eye
Fruit: black capsules, 3–6 mm long

These dainty blue flowers add fleeting beauty to damp meadows and woodland trails. Common blue-eyed grass is not a true grass but a member of the iris family. Stems of blue-eyed grass are flat or 2-sided, not round like the stems of grasses. • Dozens of blue-eyed grass species are found around the world, but some have white, yellow or purple flowers. These beautiful flowers have been much reduced by people picking them or transplanting as garden plants. They're best enjoyed by leaving them where they grow. **Where found:** moist meadows and streambanks, steppe to montane, Interior B.C.

Wood Lily

Lilium philadelphicum

Height: 30–70 cm
Leaves: 3–10 cm long; lance-shaped, whorled
Flowers: 6–10 cm wide; orange tepals with purplish dotted throats, goblet-shaped
Fruit: erect cylindrical capsules, 2–4 cm long

Almost shocking in their beauty, these brilliant orange flowers spring up along roadsides and in woodlands across much of Canada. • Native peoples ate the peppery bulbs, tiny tubers and flowers raw or cooked. The bulbs were used in poultices to heal wounds, heart problems and toothaches or were steeped into tea that was used to treat fevers or to wash sores. • Don't dig these plants out of the ground! Picking the flowers can kill the entire plant, and overzealous collectors have caused lilies to disappear in places. **Where found:** open areas (meadows, forest edges), steppe to montane, southern Interior B.C.

Nodding Onion

Allium cernuum

Height: to 50 cm
Leaves: 10–15 cm long, basal, grass-like
Flowers: 0.5 cm wide, pink to purplish, bell-shaped, nodding
Fruit: 3-lobed capsules (bulbs), 4 mm wide

When they are not in flower, wild onions are distinguished from their poisonous relative, meadow death-camas (p. 184), by their strong onion smell. Do not try the taste test. • Many Native groups and European settlers enjoyed wild onions as a vegetable and as flavouring in other foods. Cooking decreases the strong odour and makes the bulbs sweeter and easier to digest. Bears, ground squirrels and marmots also enjoy wild onions. **Where found:** dry to mesic open areas such as bluffs, open forests and meadows, steppe to montane, throughout south of 56° N.

Queen's Cup

Clintonia uniflora

Height: to 15 cm
Leaves: 7–15 cm long, basal, oblong or elliptical
Flowers: up to 2 cm wide, white, solitary
Fruit: single berry, metallic blue, to 1 cm wide

This common woodland wildflower brightens the forest floor in spring and early summer. • Although the bright metallic blue berries are unpalatable by human standards, grouse seem to enjoy them. The Bella Coola people called the fruit "wolf's berry" because it was considered only edible to wolves. • This native perennial can live for 30 or more years. **Where found:** moist to mesic forests, low to subalpine, throughout south of 56° N. **Also known as:** clintonia, bride's bonnet, corn lily.

Chocolate Lily

Fritillaria lanceolata

Height: 20–50 cm
Leaves: 5–15 cm long, 1–2 whorls of 3–5
Flowers: nodding bells, 4 cm long, single or in clusters of 2–5
Fruit: upright, 6-angled capsules with wings

The bulbs of chocolate lily are edible and were harvested and eaten by coastal Native groups. They steamed or boiled the bulbs and the slightly bitter, rice-like "bulblets." • Today, this flower is very rare and should be left undisturbed—and uneaten (see Garry oak, p. 160). Many lilies appear similar, and several are poisonous. • Northern riceroot (*F. camschatcensis*) has nodding, dark greenish-brown to purple-brown flowers and is found in moist habitats, lowland to montane. **Where found:** open grassy bluffs, meadows and woodlands, lowland to montane, B.C. south of 52° N. **Also known as:** checker lily, mission bells, *F. affinis*.

False Lily-of-the-valley

Maianthemum dilatatum

Height: 10–40 cm
Leaves: 1–3 (usually 2), alternate, heart-shaped, up to 10 cm long
Flowers: tiny, with parts in 4s, in terminal cylindrical clusters
Fruit: round berries, 6 mm across, light green to brown, maturing to red

In Haida myth, the berries were part of a feast for supernatural beings. Sometimes berries were scalded and eaten with animal or fish grease, or were stored this way. New, "folded" leaves of false lily-of-the-valley were boiled and eaten as greens in the spring by the Haida. **Where found:** mesic to wet forests and riverbanks, lowland to montane, coastal and scattered in the Interior.

Star-flowered False Solomon's-seal

Maianthemum stellatum

Height: 20–60 cm
Leaves: 5–15 cm long, lance-shaped, with prominent veins
Flowers: 5 mm wide, white, star-shaped, 5–10 in short, terminal cluster
Fruit: berries, 7–10 mm across

The species name *stellatum*, from the Latin *stella*, "star," aptly describes the radiant, white blossoms of this woodland wildflower. • This unbranched, slightly arching plant produces clusters of dark blue or reddish black berries that are greenish yellow with purplish stripes when young. • A larger relative, false Solomon's-seal (*M. racemosum*) has 5–15 cm long, puffy, pyramidal flower clusters on its showy red berries and its wavy (rather than straight-edged) leaves. **Where found:** mesic to moist forests and edges, montane to subalpine, throughout except north coast. **Also known as:** *Smilacina stellata*.

Western Trillium

Trillium ovatum

Height: to 45 cm
Leaves: 6–18 cm long, in whorls of 3
Flowers: white petals to 5 cm long
Fruit: numerous yellowish green, berry-like capsules, slightly winged

This wildflower is one of the first showy blooms to grace the forest each spring. • The ripe fruits split open to reveal many sticky seeds that contain special oily bodies called elaiosomes, which attract ants. The ants carry the seeds to their nests and bite off the "ant snack," leaving the seed to grow far from the parent plant. • Older flowers become pink or purplish, and this colour change is thought to be triggered by successful pollination: the plant is indicating to pollinating insects not to waste their time. **Where found:** moist forests, lowland to montane, south of 50° N.

Beargrass

Xerophyllum tenax

Height: up to 1.5 m
Leaves: to 90 cm long, large clumps of grass-like basal leaves; stem leaves shorter
Flowers: 1.5 cm wide, saucer-shaped, in showy white pyramidal cluster to 70 cm long
Fruit: oval 3-lobed capsules, 6 mm long

Traditionally, the tough leaves of beargrass were pounded and twisted together to make ropes and cord or were used to weave basket designs. Dried leaves turn a creamy white colour. • This plant typically flowers only once every 3 to 10 years. Often, all of the plants in a population bloom together, turning a hillside white and filling the air with a lily-like perfume. Beargrass is difficult to grow and does not do well in gardens, so it is best left in its natural habitat. • In spring, bears eat the fleshy leaf bases of this plant, thus its common name. **Where found:** dry to mesic forests and openings, montane to subalpine, southeastern B.C.

Green False-hellebore

Veratrum viride

Height: 0.7–2 m
Leaves: 10–35 cm long, large, prominently ribbed
Flowers: 1.5 cm wide, star-shaped, pale green, numerous, in terminal cluster
Fruit: brown, oblong capsules, 2 cm long

The lush, accordion-pleated leaves of green false-hellebore appear soon after snowmelt. By mid-summer, waist-high plants produce hundreds of musky-smelling flowers in long, nodding tassels. • All parts of this plant are deadly poisonous, and it is one of the most poisonous in Pacific Northwest forests. Dried plants have been used as a garden insecticide, and water from boiled roots was used to kill lice. **Where found:** moist to wet meadows, wetlands and open forests, lowland to alpine, throughout. **Also known as:** Indian hellebore, corn lily, *V. eschscholtzii*.

Meadow Death-camas

Zigadenus venenosus

Height: 40–60 cm
Leaves: up to 30 cm long
Flowers: tiny, white, saucer-shaped, in a terminal cluster 15–20 cm long
Fruit: 3-lobed capsules, 1.5 cm long

Deadly poisonous, the bulbs of this plant are very similar in appearance to those of the blue-flowered common camas (see below), which was an important food staple to Native groups and which often grows alongside death-camas. The edible variety is easily identifiable by the flowers (purple vs. white). • This plant is notorious for poisoning sheep and occasionally other livestock, but well-fed animals usually avoid it. • The toxic alkaloids cause tingling upon contact to the mouth, but ingestion results in convulsions, coma, and then death. **Where found:** mesic to dry meadows and open forests, lowland to subalpine, southern B.C. south of 52° N.

Common Camas

Camassia quamash

Height: up to 45 cm
Leaves: up to 50 cm long, basal, grass-like
Flowers: 3.5 cm wide; pale to deep blue, in terminal spike
Fruit: oval capsules, 2.5 cm long

Common camas provided a valued food and trade item to First Nations peoples in southwestern B.C. Large bulbs were harvested in late summer; smaller bulbs were left for the next year. Large harvest areas were passed for generations of families. Camas bulbs were often baked in stone pits for days until the bulbs turned dark brown, sweet and sticky, like molasses. They were then pressed into cakes and dried. **Where found:** mesic to moist meadows, lowland to montane, southwestern and southeastern B.C.

Bunchberry

Cornus canadensis

Height: 5–20 cm
Leaves: 2–8 cm long; deeply veined, in whorl of 4–6
Flowers: tiny; cluster of 5–15, surrounded by 4 white, petal-like bracts
Fruit: round, red drupes (berries), 6–8 mm across

These small flowers are really miniature bouquets of tiny blooms surrounded by showy, white petal-like bracts. The true flowers, at the centre, are easily overlooked. The large, white bracts attract and provide good landing platforms for pollinating insects. When triggered, the anthers spring out from the flower buds, catapulting pollen onto the insect or into the air. • The berry-like drupes are edible, raw or cooked. They are not very flavourful, but the crunchy, poppy-like seeds are enjoyed. **Where found:** mesic to moist sites, lowland to subalpine, throughout.

Skunk Cabbage

Lysichiton americanus

Height: 30–150 cm
Leaves: 30–120 cm long, lance-shaped, in a large, basal rosette
Flowers: tiny, greenish yellow, in a spike up to 30 cm tall
Fruit: berry-like, pulpy, green-yellow

This odd-looking arum is our first wildflower to bloom each year. As early as late February, the spathes rise up from the mire of their swampy ground, aided by an internal furnace that produces enough heat through cellular respiration to melt nearby snow and ice. The giant cabbage-like leaves emerge after flowering and persist through summer. • The smell attracts carrion-feeding and other pollinating insects but repels animals that may eat or otherwise damage the plant. **Where found:** swamps and wet forests, lowland to montane, throughout south of 56° N.

Prickly-pear

Opuntia fragilis

Height: prostrate; 5–40 cm tall
Leaves: absent; starburst cluster of spines, to 5 cm long, on 5–7 cm wide pad
Flowers: 4–8 cm wide, bell-shaped, brilliant yellow
Fruit: red-purple, fleshy, spiny, 15–25 mm long

Prickly-pear, although native here, is scattered and local, inhabiting dry, sandy areas. Watch your step! These fleshy cacti are copiously beset with spines. • Raw cacti taste like cucumber. Traditionally, once the spines and seeds were removed, the flesh was eaten raw, used to thicken stews and soups or dried for later use. More recently, the sweet flesh has been added to fruit cakes or canned as fruit juice. Berries can also be boiled whole and strained to make jellies or syrups. **Where found:** dry, open often grassy sites, lowland to montane, common in southern Interior, rare in southwest and northeast.

Western Spring-beauty

Claytonia lanceolata

Height: 5–20 cm
Leaves: 1–5 cm long, grass-like basal leaves; opposite, elliptical stem leaves
Flowers: 1 cm wide, white or pink, 5 petals with pink veins
Fruit: oval capsules

The nutritious corms of many *Claytonia* species were a valuable traditional food source. The Potato Mountains in the Chilcotin region were named after the western spring-beauty. Families camped in subalpine meadows for several weeks in late spring to dig the corms. They were collected using digging sticks or were sometimes taken from the caches of small rodents. The corms were usually cooked in pits or steamed and are said to taste like potatoes. **Where found:** moist meadows and grasslands, steppe to alpine, southern B.C.

Field Chickweed

Cerastium arvense

Height: 5–50 cm long, trailing or erect stems
Leaves: 1–3 cm long, narrow, lance-shaped
Flowers: 8–12 mm wide, white, 5 deeply notched petals
Fruit: capsules, 6–10 mm long

These open, flat-topped clusters of cheerful flowers brighten rocky mountain slopes. • The genus name *Cerastium* comes from the Greek *kerastes*, "horned," in reference to the curved, cylindrical capsules, which open by 10 small teeth at the tip. The leaves of this loosely clumped perennial often have secondary, leafy tufts in their axils. **Where found:** moist to dry open slopes and open forest, all elevations, throughout.

American Winter Cress

Barbarea orthoceras

Height: up to 80 cm
Leaves: to 12 cm long, becoming simpler and smaller higher up the stem
Flowers: 5 mm long, yellow, 4-petaled, in small terminal cluster
Fruit: seedpods (siliques), to 5 cm long

This biennial herb grows fairly tall and erect from its woody base and explodes in bright yellow flower clusters. The leaves are distinctive, with 2–3 pairs of smaller lobes and one large lobe. • *Barbarea* species were named after St. Barbara, a 4th-century saint, and were traditionally eaten on December 4, St. Barbara's Day. **Where found:** moist open areas and forests, lowland to montane, throughout.

Field Mustard

Brassica rapa

Height: 1 m
Leaves: to 12 cm long, lobed, becoming simpler and smaller higher up the stem
Flowers: yellow, 4 petals, 1 cm long
Fruit: narrow pods, up to 7 cm long

Golden fields of this introduced annual add a splash of colour to fields in spring. • Mustard plants have long been used as food and medicine. Sharp, peppery sauces (prepared mustards) are made from powdered seeds mixed with salt and vinegar. Traditionally, "plasters" of ground seeds mixed with water were applied to the chest to relieve bronchial congestion. **Caution:** mustard plasters can cause the skin to redden and blister with prolonged contact. **Where found:** disturbed sites; low to mid-elevations. **Also known as:** *B. campestris*.

186

Shepherd's Purse

Capsella bursa-pastoris

Height: up to 50 cm
Leaves: basal leaves to 6 cm long, toothed and clasping, reduced in size upward
Flowers: 3 mm long, white, numerous, clustered along stem
Fruit: flattened, triangular silicles, widest end 3 mm across

Flowers belonging to the mustard family have 4 petals in a symmetrical cross (the family was once called Cruciferae for "cross").
• This introduced species can be invasive in cultivated fields but was used in Europe for centuries as a spice and was grown for greens. All parts of shepherd's purse are edible. Young leaves may be eaten raw but are more commonly cooked in soups and stews. **Where found:** moist to dry pastures and roadsides, lowland to montane, throughout.

California Poppy

Eschscholtzia californica

Height: 10–50 cm
Leaves: 6 cm, mostly basal, highly divided (parsley-like)
Flowers: 1–5 cm wide, solitary, yellow to orange, 4 petals
Fruit: pod-like capsules

This bright and showy flower sets fields and slopes ablaze with orange and gold. The many varieties of California poppy all have a distinctive pink pedestal, like a platter with the bloom showcased atop. This plant is more noticeable once the leaves fall and only the fat, dry seedpods remain. **Where found:** dry roadsides and fields, lowland, introduced to southwestern B.C.

Common Touch-me-not

Impatiens noli-tangere

Height: 20–80 cm
Leaves: 3–12 cm long, oval, coarsely toothed
Flowers: 2.5 cm long, orange-yellow, spotted with purple, sac-like sepal
Fruit: green capsules, 2.5 cm long

This exceptionally succulent plant seems to be made from water and practically wilts before your eyes if picked. The seeds are enclosed in fleshy capsules and held by tightly coiled elastic attachments. Press a ripe pod, and the seeds shoot forth explosively, hence the name touch-me-not. The seeds taste like walnuts, and the flowers are irresistible to hummingbirds. • Crushed leaves can treat rashes caused by poison ivy and stinging nettle, and leaf poultices are said to counteract dermatitis, insect bites and warts. **Where found:** moist forests and wetlands, lowland to montane, throughout.
Also known as: jewelweed.

Northern Bedstraw

Galium boreale

Height: 20–60 cm
Leaves: 2–6 cm long; narrow, in whorls of 4
Flowers: 4–7 mm across; white, in clusters
Fruit: paired nutlets, less than 1.5–2 mm across

Bedstraws are related to coffee, and their tiny, paired, short and hairy nutlets can be dried, roasted and ground as a coffee substitute. • Bedstraw juice or tea was once applied to many skin problems. Today, some people drink the tea to speed weight loss, but continual use irritates the mouth, and people with poor circulation or diabetes should not use it. • The flowers are arranged in repeatedly 3-forked clusters. • Sweet-scented bedstraw (*G. triflorum*) has whorls of 5–6 broader, bristle-tipped leaves, and its nutlets are covered with long, hooked bristles. **Where found:** moist to dry open areas and open forests, lowland to subalpine, throughout except for Haida Gwaii and north coast.

Common Harebell

Campanula rotundifolia

Height: 10–50 cm
Leaves: 1–6 cm long; stem leaves narrow; basal leaves rounded
Flowers: 2 cm long, purple-blue, bell-shaped
Fruit: capsules, 5–8 mm long

From open woodlands to exposed, rocky slopes, these delicate, nodding bells bob in the breeze on thin, wiry stems. • The small openings at the base of the capsules close quickly in damp weather, protecting the seeds from excess moisture. On dry, windy days, the capsules swing widely in the breeze, scattering the seeds. • The species name *rotundifolia* refers to this plant's round, basal leaves. **Where found:** mesic to dry meadows and openings, lowland to alpine, throughout.

Small-flowered Woodland Star

Lithophragma parviflorum

Height: 10–40 cm
Leaves: 2–5 cm wide, basal, kidney-shaped but deeply divided
Flowers: 1 cm across, white to pink, in cluster up to 15 cm long
Fruit: 3-chambered capsules

Caught up in a breeze, these star-like flowers atop their slender stems sway like magic wands conducting spells across the meadows. The white, pink or lavender flowers have 5 petals, each with 3 lobes, and are closely attached to the stems. • This flower makes its appearance in spring on wooded foothills where, typical of the saxifrage family, it finds its preferred rocky habitat. **Where found:** mesic to dry meadows, bluffs and open forests, lowland to montane, southern B.C.

Brook Saxifrage

Saxifraga odontoloma

Height: inflorescence 15–30 cm
Leaves: up to 20 cm long, basal, toothed
Flowers: 5 mm across, 5 petals
Fruit: capsules, 5 mm long

Saxifrage means "stone breaker," referring to the preference of some species for rocky habitats such as mountain ridges or even stone walls. • Brook saxifrage displays all the characteristics of a typical saxifrage: a leafless stem rising above large, round, basal, scallop-toothed leaves and many gracefully hanging flowers with spade-shaped white petals and contrasting yellow dots. **Where found:** streambanks and other moist, shady spots, montane to subalpine, throughout but most common in southwestern B.C.

Three-leaved Foamflower

Tiarella trifoliata

Height: 15–60 cm
Leaves: mainly basal, to 12 cm wide, divided into 3 short-stemmed, coarsely toothed leaflets
Flowers: 6–10 mm across, in clusters on wiry stalks
Fruit: capsules resemble sugar scoops

Delicate white flowers atop slender stems and broad, maple-like leaves characterize this abundant plant. The flowers look like flecks of foam, hence the plant's name. • When the fruits mature, the capsules split open to resemble sugar scoops and sprinkle out tiny, black seeds. **Where found:** moist forests and meadows, lowland to subalpine, throughout south of 58° N. **Also known as:** sugar scoop.

Lance-leaved Stonecrop

Sedum lanceolatum

Height: 5–20 cm
Leaves: 1 cm long, lance-shaped, fleshy
Flowers: 1 cm long, yellow, in flat-topped clusters
Fruit: erect follicles

These small, hardy perennials grace rugged slopes with flashes of bright yellow. Their succulent, green or reddish leaves (sometimes coated with a whitish, waxy powder) and low growth-form help them to survive in dry, rocky sites. Many stonecrops are cultivated in rock gardens or as house plants. **Where found:** dry, stony, open sites from plains to alpine zones; southern B.C.

Common Plantain

Plantago major

Height: up to 60 cm
Leaves: 5–18 cm
Flowers: 5–30 cm clusters
Fruit: capsules, 2–4 mm

Common plantain sprouts up on just about any disturbed ground, and you've probably tried to rid this common weed from your lawn without realizing its uses. This nutritious plant is high in vitamins A, C and K and is said to taste like Swiss chard. The young leaves may be eaten raw, but tough, mature leaves are best chopped fine and cooked. Dried, ground seeds can be used as flour. Plantain leaves may be steeped into a hair rinse to prevent dandruff. The strong veins of mature leaves were traditionally used as thread and fishing line. **Where found:** mesic to dry lawns and other disturbed areas, lowland to montane, throughout inhabited areas.

Cut-leaf Anemone

Anemone multifida

Height: 15–60 cm
Leaves: to 5 cm long; divided into 3 leaflets, each divided 2–3 times
Flowers: 2 cm wide; white, yellowish or pink
Fruit: woolly achenes, borne in 1 cm wide oval clusters

A burst of yellow stamens and 5–8 white, yellow or pink sepals, sometimes tinged with purple or red, are the showy parts of this flower, which doesn't actually have true petals. After the flowers fade, the woolly, spherical fruits look like wind-tousled heads. "Anemone" comes from the Greek word for "wind"; these flowers are sometimes called windflowers. **Where found:** rocky areas in mid to high elevations; open woods and rocky meadows elsewhere; throughout.

Western Columbine

Aquilegia formosa

Height: up to 1 m
Leaves: variable, usually twice divided into 3s, to 5 cm long
Flowers: 3 cm long; nodding, tubular, red and yellow petals with 5 red spurs
Fruit: 5 erect follicles with hairy, spreading tips

Striking, colourful columbine flowers entice hummingbirds and long-tongued butterflies, which then pollinate the plants. • The common name means "dove," and the Latin name *Aquilegia* means "eagle." Both names refer to the yellow, talon-like spurs of the flowers. • The Haida had a superstition that picking these flowers would bring on rain, while other Native groups considered the flower a good luck charm. **Where found:** mesic to moist clearings and open forests, lowland to subalpine, throughout. **Also known as:** crimson columbine, red columbine.

Marsh Marigold

Caltha leptosepala

Height: 5–30 cm
Leaves: to 6 cm long, basal
Flowers: 2–4 cm wide, white or greenish
Fruit: up to 2 cm long, beaked, bright yellow-green, in a cluster of 3–8

This species has a few distinctive, eye-catching characteristics that help to identify it. Marsh marigold has
large, fleshy basal leaves, 5–10 or more showy, white
sepals and many bright yellow-green stamens and pistils
clumped in the centre of the flower. **Where found:** wetlands and
seepage sites, lowland to alpine, throughout except Haida Gwaii
and adjacent mainland coast. **Also known as:** alpine white marsh-marigold.

Western Buttercup

Ranunculus occidentalis

Height: 15–60 cm
Leaves: 2.5–8 cm long, basal leaves 3-wedged, coarsely toothed,
smaller stem leaves
Flowers: 1–2.5 cm wide, yellow, 5–8 petals
Fruit: spherical head of 5–20 tiny achenes

"Butter" only goes as far as the colour, not to any culinary uses—this plant
is poisonous to people and livestock. However, buttercup essence is popular
and is derived for use in holistic treatments. It is said to help the soul realize
its inner light and beauty. • Traditionally, the toxic sap was applied to warts or
plague sores, and the juice was used to irritate the skin to counteract arthritis
and nerve pain. • The name *Ranunculus* is Latin for "little frog." **Where found:** moist
to mesic grassy meadows, bluffs and open forests, lowland to subalpine, throughout.

Western Meadowrue

Thalictrum occidentale

Height: 40–100 cm
Leaves: 1–5 cm long, divided 3–4 times into 3s
Flowers: 2–4 mm long; greenish, in many-flowered clusters
Fruit: seed-like achenes, 3–5 mm long

Tiny meadowrue flowers appear in showy, pyramid-shaped clusters.
Plants are usually either male or female. Male flowers have dangling
purplish anthers, and the less showy, greenish female flowers give way
to small fruit. • Dried seeds and leaves may be used as a fragrant pot-
pourri. The pleasant-smelling plants and seeds were burned in smudges or
stored with possessions as insect repellent and perfume. **Where found:** moist
to mesic open areas and open forests, lowland to subalpine, throughout
except Haida Gwaii, northern Vancouver Is. and adjacent coastlines.

191

Virginia Strawberry

Fragaria virginiana

Height: 5–15 cm
Leaves: 5–10 cm long; divided into 3 coarsely toothed leaflets
Flowers: 1.5–2 cm wide; white, 5 petals
Fruit: red strawberry dotted with achenes

Few things beat running into a patch of fresh, wild strawberries. They are delicious, but many other animals know that—good luck beating them to the crop. This plant is the ancestor of 90% of our cultivated strawberries. Each tiny red berry contains all the flavour of a large domestic strawberry. The rhizomes and runners produce tufts of bluish-tinged leaves with 3-toothed leaflets. **Where found:** dry fields and open woods.

Canada Violet

Viola canadensis

Height: up to 40 cm
Leaves: 5–10 cm long; broadly heart-shaped
Flowers: 2 cm wide; white with yellow centre and purple veins, 5 petals
Fruit: capsules with tiny dark seeds

Of all our native violets, Canada violet is perhaps the most stately and handsome. This species has tall, upright stems and bright white flowers with lemon-yellow centres. Seeds are often dispersed by ants that carry them to their nests then bite off the elaiosome bodies—oily, tasty "ant snacks." • Violet flowers make a pretty garnish for salads, and the cooked or raw leaves are high in vitamins A and C. **Caution:** seeds and rhizomes are poisonous. • Yellow, white and blue-flowered violet species are widespread across our region, including early blue violet *(V. adunca),* found on sandy soils. **Where found:** damp woods.

Arctic Lupine

Lupinus arcticus

Height: up to 80 cm
Leaves: 3–6 cm long, with 6–8 palmately arranged leaflets
Flowers: 12–15 mm long, bluish, pea-like, in dense elongate clusters
Fruit: hairy seedpods, turning blackish, to 4 cm long

Few botanical sights are more fetching than a blanket of flowering lupine, their bright blue blossoms splashing colour on barren subalpine slopes. Lupines enrich the soil with nitrogen and attract butterflies. These plants can be especially dangerous because their poisonous pods look like hairy garden peas, and children may assume that they are edible. **Where found:** moist to mesic openings and open forests, all elevations, throughout.

Red Clover

Trifolium pratense

Height: 80 cm
Leaves: 2–5 cm; 3 leaflets
Flowers: 25–35 mm long; pink to purple, in dense clusters
Fruit: 1-seeded pods

A ubiquitous weedy plant of open ground, red clover has round, pink to purple flowerheads and large leaves. • Native to Europe, red clover is widely used around the world as fodder. It depends on bumble bees for pollination, so when clover crops were introduced to Australia, bumble bees were imported, too. Red clovers are heavily used by native butterflies. Clouded sulphurs nectar at the blossoms and probably use red clover as a host plant. **Where found:** open, disturbed sites such as roadsides, fields, lawns; throughout.

American Vetch

Vicia americana

Height: 20–100 cm
Leaves: 2–3 cm long; compound, 8–18 oblong leaflets
Flowers: 2 cm long; bluish purple, pea-like, in clusters
Fruit: pods, 2–3 cm long

Twining tendrils wrap around nearby stems and leaves as this slender vine climbs upward over its neighbours. Its flat, hairless "pea pods" are attractive to children, but they are not edible. • When an insect lands on a vetch flower, anthers spring out to dust the insect's belly with pollen. The next flower collects the pollen on its stigma and applies another load of pollen. **Where found:** mesic to moist open forests, meadows and streamsides, lowland to montane, throughout but absent from Haida Gwaii.

Stinging Nettle

Urtica dioica

Height: 1–3 m
Leaves: 4–15 cm long; coarsely toothed
Flowers: 1–2 mm long; green to purplish, in drooping clusters
Fruit: achenes, 1–2 mm long

The stinging hairs on the stems and undersides of this plant's leaves contain formic acid and can cause itching and burning. The sting lasts 10 minutes to several days, depending on how sensitive you are. • Some people use gloves to pick young, tender nettles to make soup or steam them as a delicious spring vegetable. Cooking destroys the acid, but eating large amounts may cause stomach irritation. **Where found:** moist to mesic floodplains, avalanche tracks, open deciduous forests and other open areas, lowland to subalpine, throughout.

193

Common Fireweed

Epilobium angustifolium

Height: 3 m (occasionally taller)
Leaves: 2–20 cm long; lance-shaped
Flowers: 1–3 cm wide; pink to purple, in long, erect clusters
Fruit: narrow, pod-like capsules, 4–8 cm long

Aptly named, fireweed reaches peak abundance immediately after fires and can turn freshly scarred landscapes pink with its blooms. Not surprisingly, this plant is a dominant feature of innumerable photographs of northern landscapes. Fireweed serves an important ecological role by stabilizing barren ground, which eventually allows other species of plants to recolonize. The erect, linear pods split lengthwise to release hundreds of tiny seeds tipped with fluffy, white hairs (comas). • Young shoots can be eaten like asparagus, and the flowers can be added to salads. **Where found:** burns, roadsides, meadows and other open areas, all elevations, throughout.

Common Cow-parsnip

Heracleum maximum

Height: 1–3 m
Leaves: 10–40 cm long; compound, divided into 3 large, toothed leaflets
Flowers: small, in flat-topped clusters 10–20 cm across
Fruit: seed-like schizocarps, 7–12 mm across

The young, fleshy stems of cow-parsnip can be peeled and eaten raw or cooked. They are said to taste like celery, but do not confuse cow-parsnip with the deadly poisonous water-hemlocks. Many animals, including bears, eat cow-parsnip. • Toy flutes or whistles can be made from the dry, hollow stems, but they may irritate the lips and cause painful blisters, leading to a medical condition known as "pea-shooter syndrome." **Where found:** moist to wet meadows, marshes, open forests, all elevations, throughout.

Northern Gentian

Gentianella amarella

Height: 10–40 cm
Leaves: 5 cm long, elliptical, in pairs
Flowers: 2 cm long, violet to pinkish, tubular with fringed petals
Fruit: capsules

The flowers of this late bloomer stand up to the first frosts. Before the widespread introduction of hops, gentians were used in Europe for brewing beers. • Gentian roots have been used in many forms to treat various ailments and in bitter tonics that aid digestion. Present-day herbalists recommend gentian-root tea as one of the best vegetable bitters for stimulating appetite, aiding digestion, relieving bloating and preventing heartburn. **Where found:** moist meadows, open forests and other openings, lowland to montane, common in the Interior, less common on the coast. **Also known as:** felwort.

Bracted Lousewort

Pedicularis bracteosa

Height: to 1 m
Leaves: to 15 cm long, elliptical, deeply divided, fern-like
Flowers: 1 cm long, yellow or bicoloured, hooded, in spike
Fruit: dry capsules, 3 mm long

Odd-looking with fern-like leaves, lousewort flowers are striking for their irregular shapes. This plant depends on a special root fungi for nutrient intake and should not be transplanted or disturbed because it will not survive. • It was once thought that if cattle consumed this plant, they would become louse-ridden, hence the name. **Where found:** moist meadows and open forests, montane to alpine, throughout south of 56° N.

Spreading Phlox

Phlox diffusa

Height: 5–10 cm, mat-forming
Leaves: 0.5–2 cm long, paired
Flowers: 9–17 mm wide, white, pink or bluish, solitary
Fruit: 3-chambered capsules

This phlox is named for its bright, spreading flowers and beautiful way of carpeting the ground with dense greenery. Phlox have long corolla tubes, which butterflies and moths with long tongues are perfectly adapted to pollinate. **Where found:** mesic to dry rocky slopes and open forests, all elevations, common in southwestern B.C., less common in south central and southeast.

Tall Bluebells

Mertensia paniculata

Height: 20–150 cm
Leaves: 3–15 cm, elliptic to oblanceolate
Flowers: 8–15 mm long, pale blue (sometimes pink), bell-shaped
Fruit: 4 wrinkled nutlets, 2.5–5 mm long

Bluebell flowers change colour as they grow. Flower buds are pink, becoming blue as the flowers open and mature, then fading to pink or almost white with age. This colour change may serve to attract insects only when flowers are receptive, because the majority of northern insects are attracted to blue but are "blind" to red. • The name *Mertensia* honours Franz Karl Mertens, a renowned German botanist who primarily collected algae. **Where found:** mesic to wet meadows and open forests, subalpine and alpine, common in northern B.C., less common in the south.

195

Scarlet Paintbrush

Castilleja miniata

Height: 20–60 cm
Leaves: 5–7 cm; lance-shaped, 3-lobed tip
Flowers: 2–3 cm long; tubular, hidden by showy scarlet bracts
Fruit: capsules, 9–12 mm long

It is usually easy to recognize a paintbrush but difficult to say which of the 150–200 species you have. *Castilleja* is a confusing genus, with many flower shapes and colours, and its species often hybridize. Paintbrushes join roots with nearby plants to steal nutrients, and many depend on their neighbours for sustenance. Showy, red bracts give these flower clusters their colour. The tubular flowers are greenish with a short, broad lower lip and a long, slender upper lip that is over half as long as the tube. **Where found:** wet to dry meadows, wetlands and open forests, lowland to subalpine, throughout.

Yellow Monkeyflower

Mimulus guttatus

Height: 10–80 cm
Leaves: to 5 cm long, in pairs
Flowers: 2–4 cm long, yellow, trumpet-shaped
Fruit: oblong capsules, 1–2 cm long

Hold one of the flowers to your face and look at it head-on, and there is a resemblance to a monkey, hence the common name. *Mimulus* is the diminutive form of the Latin *mimus,* meaning a buffoon or actor in a farce or mime, an apparent reference to the small, grinning, ape-like faces of the blossoms. This relative of snapdragons brightens moist open habitats with yellow blooms. **Where found:** wet seepage areas, meadows and other open areas, lowland to subalpine, throughout.

Davidson's Penstemon

Penstemon davidsonii

Height: 5–10 cm, mat-forming
Leaves: 5–15 mm long, evergreen, thick
Flowers: 25–35 mm long, tubular, purple to blue-lavender
Fruit: narrowly winged capsules, 8–10 mm long

The richly purple to blue-lavender flowers are relatively large compared to the small evergreen leaves and low growth-form of this plant. Five petals unite into long, 2-lipped tubes that stand out like loud purple trumpets among the drab-coloured rocks that are this plant's preferred habitat. The throats and anthers of the showy flowers are woolly. **Where found:** dry, rocky sites, montane to alpine, throughout south of 55° N. **Also known as:** alpine penstemon.

American Brooklime

Veronica americana

Height: 10–70 cm
Leaves: to 5 cm long
Flowers: 5 mm wide, saucer-shaped
Fruit: tiny round capsules

The leaves of American brooklime are edible and commonly used in salads or as a potherb. Because it most often grows directly in water, be sure not to collect the leaves from plants in polluted sites. • The showy flowers are blue to violet, sometimes white, with red-purple markings and 2 large, reaching stamens that look like antennae. **Where found:** wetlands and stream edges, lowland to montane, throughout. **Also known as:** American speedwell.

Common Yarrow

Achillea millefolium

Height: 30–90 cm
Leaves: 5–15 cm long; feathery appearance
Flowers: less than 7 mm long; white, in flat-topped cluster
Fruit: compressed achenes

The fern-like leaves of this member of the sunflower family (Asteraceae) are distinctive. Yarrow is often weedy, and both native and introduced populations occur in our region. • This hardy, aromatic perennial has served for thousands of years as a fumigant, insecticide and medicine. The Greek hero Achilles, for whom the genus was named, used it to help heal his soldiers' wounds. • Yarrow is an attractive ornamental, but beware—its extensive underground stems (rhizomes) soon invade your garden. **Where found:** moist to dry open areas and open forests, all elevations, throughout.

Arrow-leaved Groundsel

Senecio triangularis

Height: 30–150 cm
Leaves: 5–15 cm long, triangular, toothed
Flowers: 1–2 cm wide; yellow, in flat-topped cluster
Fruit: seed-like achenes, tipped with fluffy white hairs

One of the largest and most diverse genera in the world, *Senecio* contains more than 30 species in B.C. and 77 species in North America. Large, triangular-shaped leaves and yellow flowers help to identify arrow-leaved groundsel. • *Senecio* comes from the Latin *senex*, or "old man," referring to the fuzzy seedheads. **Where found:** mesic to wet meadows and other open areas, and open forests, all elevations, throughout.

Leafy Aster

Symphyotrichum foliaceum

Height: 20–60 cm
Leaves: 5–12 cm long, oval or lance-shaped, sometimes clasping at base
Flowers: ray flowers 1–2 cm long; disk flowers tiny, yellow
Fruit: hairy achenes

These cheerful, purplish asters beautify many of our trails, clearings and roadsides. The yellow disk flowers in the centre of the inflorescence are surrounded by ray flowers that can range in colour from white to blue to pink, purple or red. • The name "aster" means "star" and refers to the shape of the flowers. **Where found:** moist to mesic openings and forests, all elevations, throughout (less common in the north). **Also known as:** leafy-headed aster, *Aster foliaceus.*

Subalpine Fleabane

Erigeron peregrinus

Height: 10–70 cm
Leaves: 1–20 cm long, highly variable, lance to spoon-shaped
Flowers: 2–6 cm wide, pink, purplish or lavender
Fruit: hairy achenes

These star-like flowerheads often appear in Native basketry patterns. Fleabanes are easily confused with asters. Aster flowerheads usually have overlapping rows of bracts (involucral bracts) with light, parchment-like bases and green tips. Fleabanes usually have one row of slender bracts with the same texture and colour (not green) throughout. Also, fleabanes generally flower earlier and have narrower, more numerous rays. Subalpine fleabane has glandular involucral bracts, and its seed-like fruits are white to tan with hair-like parachutes. **Where found:** moist to wet open areas at all elevations, throughout.

Heart-leaved Arnica

Arnica cordifolia

Height: 10–60 cm
Leaves: 4–10 cm long, heart-shaped, coarsely toothed
Flowers: 2.5–6 cm across, yellow with central "button"
Fruit: 6.5–8 mm long, hairy achenes

These cheerful, yellow wildflowers were once used in love charms because of their heart-shaped leaves. Rootstocks and flowers were used in washes and poultices for treating bruises, sprains and swollen feet, but these poisonous plants are never applied to broken skin. This single-stemmed perennial produces seed-like fruits with tufts of white, hair-like bristles. **Where found:** mesic to dry forests and meadows, montane to alpine, common in the Interior, rare on the coast.

Canada Thistle

Cirsium arvense

Height: 30–150 cm
Leaves: 5–15 cm long, spiny-toothed
Flowers: disk flowers pink-purple, in heads 15–25 mm across
Fruit: seed-like achenes

Canada thistle was introduced to Canada from Europe in the 17th century, then expanded its range into the United States, where it acquired its common name. Today, this aggressive weed is found in virtually all croplands and pastures. Prickly thistle colonies grow from deep underground runners that contain tricin, which inhibits the growth of nearby plants. Each year, one plant can send out up to 6 m of runners, and female plants can release up to 40,000 seeds. • The flowers provide a good source of pollen and nectar for honeybees, and humans can eat the shoots and roots. **Where found:** mesic to dry openings and waste places, lowland to montane, common throughout.

Canada Goldenrod

Solidago canadensis

Height: 30–120 cm
Leaves: 5–10 cm long, lance-shaped
Flowers: tiny; ray and disk flowers, in pyramidal clusters
Fruit: hairy, seed-like achenes

Many people blame these bold, pyramid-shaped flower clusters for causing allergies, but the real culprit is probably a less conspicuous plant, such as ragweed (*Ambrosia* spp.), which shares the same habitat. Goldenrod pollen is too heavy to be carried by the wind; instead, it is carried by flying insects. • Each seed-like fruit is tipped with parachutes of white hairs. **Where found:** mesic to moist openings and waste places, lowland to montane, common throughout.

Coltsfoot

Petasites frigidus

Height: 10–50 cm
Leaves: 10–30 cm long; basal; variable arrow-shaped, rounded or deeply lobed
Flowers: 8 mm across; white to pinkish, in dense, rounded cluster
Fruit: seed-like achenes, 2–3 mm long, with a tuft of white, hair-like bristles

The coltsfoots, though very different in appearance because of their distinctive leaf shapes, are now considered varieties of one species, *P. frigidus*. • The salt-rich ash of coltsfoot leaves were once widely used as a salt substitute. Dried coltsfoot has been used for hundreds of years to make medicinal teas to relieve coughing and pain from chest colds, whooping cough, asthma and viral pneumonia. Pregnant women should not eat this plant. **Where found:** moist to wet open areas (streambanks, meadows) and open forests, all elevations, throughout.

Sitka Valerian

Valeriana sitchensis

Height: 30–70 cm
Leaves: 5–8 cm long, opposite, in 3–5 coarsely toothed, oval leaflets
Flowers: 4 mm wide; long, white to pale pink, in rounded clusters
Fruit: egg-shaped, ribbed achenes, 3–6 mm long

Dried, frozen or bruised valerian plants have a strong, unpleasant smell. Sitka valerian is responsible for the sour odour detected in subalpine meadows after the first frost. The ornamental valerian flowers are appreciated in gardens and attract butterflies and hummingbirds. **Where found:** moist meadows, avalanche tracks and open forests, montane to alpine, throughout.

Yellow Pond-lily

Nuphar lutea

Leaves: 7–35 cm
Flowers: 35–60 mm
Fruit: spongy berries, 20–45 mm

This floating, aquatic perennial grows from a large, buried rootstock. Some Native groups sliced the rootstocks and ate them fried or boiled, or dried and ground them into flour, but other groups considered them inedible. If eaten in large amounts, pond-lily rootstocks can be potentially poisonous. Dried, sliced rootstocks were made into medicinal teas and used to treat arthritis, headaches, sore throats and heart problems or to aid in childbirth. **Where found:** ponds, lowland to montane, B.C. south of 55° N.

Common Cattail

Typha latifolia

Height: up to 3 m
Leaves: up to 3 m long, up to 2 cm wide; linear
Flowers: tiny, yellowish green, in dense spikes 8–14 cm long
Fruit: tiny; achenes in fuzzy brown spike (cattail)

Cattails rim wetlands and line lakeshores and ditches across North America, providing cover for many animals. They are critical for supporting least bitterns, marsh wrens and other marsh birds. • Cattails grow from long rhizomes that were traditionally eaten fresh in spring. Later in the season, when the rhizomes became bitter, they were peeled and roasted, or dried and ground into flour. • Fresh, dried seedheads were used to bandage burns and promote healing. **Where found:** shallow open water, lowland to montane, throughout.

Needle-and-thread Grass

Hesperostipa comata

Height: 30–70 cm
Leaves: 10–30 cm; wide, flat, rolled in
Flowers: long, curled, thread-like awns
Fruit: pointed seed fruits

There are hundreds of grass species in B.C., mostly with stems that are round in cross-section and hollow. Sedges and rushes (see below) can resemble grasses but have stems that are solid (not hollow) in cross-section. • Needle-and-thread grass is named for its thread-like awns and slender, pointed, needle-like seed fruits. The hygroscropic awns wind and unwind with changes in temperature and moisture, drilling the pointed seeds into the soil to increase their chances of germinating. Bunches grow from a deep root system. **Where found:** dry, grassy open areas, steppe to montane, south central and southeastern B.C.

Water Sedge

Carex aquatilis

Height: clumps to 1 m tall
Leaves: grass-like, 3–7 mm wide
Flowers: terminal spikes of tiny male flowers, lower spikes of tiny female flowers
Fruit: brownish-green egg-shaped perigynia, 2–4 mm long

B.C. has more than 150 species of sedges, mostly with stems that are triangular in cross-section and solid (not hollow like grasses). Remember: "sedges have edges, and rushes are round." B.C.'s sedges range from tall plants (like this one) that can grow to more than 1 m tall, to tiny species no more than 15 cm tall, and occupy terrestrial and aquatic habitats from sea level to alpine. Water sedge is one of a group of tall, aquatic sedges that provide important habitat and food for aquatic wildlife. **Where found:** wetlands and lakeshores, all elevations, throughout.

Common Rush

Juncus effusus

Height: dense clusters of stems to 1 m tall
Leaves: short sheaths only, at stem base
Flowers: tiny brownish flowers on lateral branched clusters off the stem
Fruit: egg-shaped capsules, about 3 mm long

B.C. has almost 50 species of rushes *(Juncus),* mostly with stems that are round in cross-section and solid (not hollow like grasses). The stems of common rush were used by First Nations peoples for weaving mats, though some considered them too brittle and preferred to use sedge or grass leaves. **Where found:** moist to wet wetlands and other openings, forest edges, lowland to montane, common on the coast, less common in the Interior.

Scouler's Surfgrass

Phyllospadix scouleri

Height: submerged marine perennial, 5–50 cm long
Leaves: flat, grass-like, 2–4 mm wide, to 150 cm long
Flowers: stalked spikes of male or female flowers
Fruit: 3–4 mm long nutlets

Not algae, not grass, but a type of flowering plant, surfgrass is one of the few flowering plants that are truly marine. It spends almost its entire life underwater, rarely exposed at low tide, when long, narrow, bright green strands can be seen in shallow, rocky waters. • Flowers are tiny and inconspicuous because there is no need to attract insects for pollination. Pollen is released in long, thread-like strands and carried by water currents. The seeds are dispersed by waves. **Where found:** rocky coasts exposed to wave action, all along B.C.'s coast.

Common Horsetail

Equisetum arvense

Height: up to 50 cm
Leaves: small scales
Spore clusters: blue-tipped cones

Next time you come across a horsetail, feel the stem. Silica crystals cause the rough texture and strengthen the plant. First Nations peoples used the abrasive horsetails like sandpaper to smooth tools. • Most people are familiar with this plant's sterile "horsetail" stems that have many whorls of slender branches, but common horsetail also sprouts unbranched, fertile stems that are often overlooked. These smaller, brownish shoots have blunt cones at their tips and look similar to slender mushrooms. **Where found:** mesic to wet sites, open or forested, all elevations, throughout.

Bracken Fern

Pteridium aquilinum

Height: fronds up to 1 m
Leaves: blades triangular, 10 or more leaflets

Pioneers of recently disturbed open sites, bracken ferns sometimes form sizeable colonies from creeping root systems. They flourish in dry sandy soil. Their success is aided by allelopathic chemicals exuded through the roots, which inhibit the growth of competing plants. This fern occurs on nearly every continent. • Bracken fern's 2- to 3-times divided pinnate leaves form a triangle. Like many other ferns, lines of brown spore cases dot the undersides of the leaves. • **Caution:** bracken ferns are carcinogenic to humans and animals and should be treated with caution. **Where found:** dry to wet open areas and forest edges, lowland to subalpine, B.C. south of 55° N.

Sword Fern

Polystichum munitum

Height: up to 1.5 m
Leaves: blades lance-shaped, many leaflets

Plants in the genus *Polystichum* are all large, tufted, evergreen ferns that form crown-like bunches from a single woody rhizome. The sword fern is one of several *Polystichum* species in our area. • This plant was used by Native groups for lining pit ovens, wrapping and storing food, flooring and bedding. • These ferns have large, circular sori (groups of spore sacs) on the undersides of the leaflets. **Where found:** moist to wet forests, lowland to montane, common on coast, less common in Interior.

Maidenhair Fern

Adiantum aleuticum

Height: 15–60 cm
Leaves: palmate, many leaflets

Though it grows in colonies and can appear lush, this delicate fern typically has a single or very few palmately branched leaves on thin, dark brown or purple-black stems. • This fern was often used in Native basketry as well as medicinally. It was exported to Europe and used in herbal cough medicines. **Where found:** moist forests and rich rock faces, often in waterfall spray zones, lowland to montane, throughout but more common in the south.

GLOSSARY

A

achene: a seed-like fruit, e.g., sunflower seed

alcids: a family of birds that includes puffins, murrelets, auklets and other similar birds

algae: simple photosynthetic aquatic plants lacking true stems, roots, leaves and flowers, and ranging in size from single-celled forms to giant kelp

altricial: animals that are helpless at birth or hatching

ammocetes: larval lamprey

anadromous: fish that migrate from salt water to fresh water to spawn

annual: plants that live for only 1 year or growing season

anterior: situated at or toward the front

aquatic: water frequenting

arboreal: tree frequenting

autotrophic: an organism that produces its own food, e.g., by photosynthesis

B

barbels: fleshy, whisker-like appendages found on some fish

basal leaf: a leaf arising from the base of a plant

benthic: bottom feeding

berry: a fleshy fruit, usually with several to many seeds

bivalve: a group of molluscs in which the animal is enclosed by 2 valves (shells)

bract: a leaf-like structure arising from the base of a flower or inflorescence

bracteole: a small bract borne on a leaf stalk

brood parasite: a bird that parasitizes other bird's nests by laying its eggs and then abandoning them for the parasitized birds to raise, e.g., brown-headed cowbird

bulb: a fleshy underground organ with overlapping, swollen scales, e.g., an onion

C

calyx: a collective term for the sepals of a flower

cambium: inner layers of tissue that transport nutrients up and down the plant stalk or trunk

canopy: the fairly continuous cover provided by the branches and leaves of adjacent trees

capsules: a dry fruit that splits open to release seeds

carapace: a protective bony shell (e.g., of a turtle) or exoskeleton (e.g., of beetles)

carnivorous: feeding primarily on meat

carrion: decomposing animal matter; a carcass

catkin: a spike of small flowers

chelipeds: the clawed first pair of legs, e.g., on a crab

compound leaf: a leaf separated into 2 or more divisions called leaflets

cone: the fruit produced by a coniferous plant, composed of overlapping scales around a central axis

coniferous: cone-bearing; seed (female) and pollen (male) cones are borne on the same tree in different locations

corm: a swollen underground stem base used by some plants as an organ of propagation; resembles a bulb

crepuscular: active primarily at dusk and dawn

cryptic colouration: a colouration pattern designed to conceal an animal

D

deciduous: a tree whose leaves turn colour and are shed annually

defoliating: dropping of the leaves

disk flower: a small flower in the centre, or disk, of a composite flower (e.g., aster, daisy or sunflower)

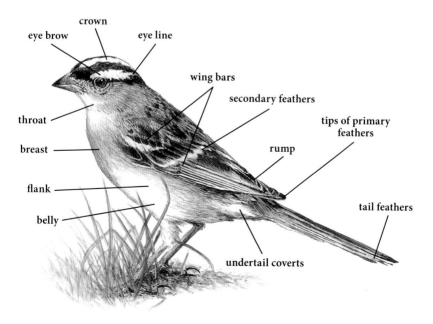

diurnal: active primarily during the day

dorsal: the top or back

drupe: a fleshy fruit with a stony pit, e.g., peach, cherry

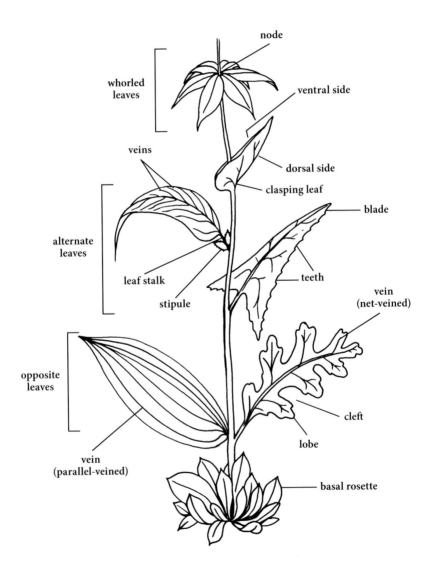

E

echolocation: navigation by rebounding sound waves off objects to target or avoid them

ecological niche: an ecological role filled by a species

ecoregion: distinction between regions based upon geology, climate, biodiversity, elevation and soil composition

ectoparasites: skin parasites

ectotherm: an animal that regulates its body temperature behaviourally from external sources of heat, i.e., from the sun

eft: the stage of a newt's life following the tadpole stage, in which it exits the water and leads a terrestrial life; when the newt matures to adulthood it returns to the water

endotherm: an animal that regulates its body temperature internally

estivate: a state of inactivity and a slowing of the metabolism to permit survival in extended periods of high temperatures and inadequate water supply

estuarine: an area where a freshwater river exits into the sea; the salinity of the seawater drops because it is diluted by the fresh water

eutrophic: a nutrient-rich body of water with an abundance of algae growth and a low level of dissolved oxygen

evergreen: having green leaves through winter; not deciduous

exoskeleton: a hard outer encasement that provides protection and points of attachment for muscles

F

flight membrane: the membrane between the fore and hind limbs of bats and some squirrels that allows bats to fly and squirrels to glide through the air

follicle: the structure in the skin from which hair or feathers grow; a dry fruit that splits open along a single line on one side when ripe; a cocoon

food web: the elaborated, interconnected feeding relationships of living organisms in an ecosystem

forb: a broad-leaved plant that lacks a permanent woody stem and loses its aboveground growth each year; may be annual, biennial or perennial

fry: a newly hatched fish that has used up its yolk sac and has commenced active feeding

G

gillrakers: long, thin, fleshy projections that protect delicate gill tissue from particles in the water

glandular: similar to or containing glands

H

habitat: the physical area in which an organism lives

hawking: feeding behaviour in which a bird leaves a perch, snatches its prey in midair, and then returns to its previous perch

herbaceous: feeding primarily on vegetation

hibernation: a state of decreased metabolism and body temperature and slowed heart and respiratory rates to permit survival during long periods of cold temperature and diminished food supply

hibernaculum: a shelter in which an animal, usually a mammal, reptile or insect, chooses to hibernate

hind: female elk (this term is used mostly in Asia—in North America "cow" is more often used)

hips: the berry-like fruit of some plants in the rose family (Rosaceae)

holdfast: the root-like structure that seaweeds use to hold onto rocky substrates

hybrids: the offspring from a cross between parents belonging to different varieties or subspecies, sometimes between different subspecies or genera

I

incubate: to keep eggs at a relatively constant temperature until they hatch

inflorescence: a cluster of flowers on a stalk; may be arranged as a spike, raceme, head, panicle, etc.

insectivorous: feeding primarily on insects

intertidal zone: the area between low- and high-tide lines

invertebrate: any animal lacking a backbone, e.g., worms, slugs, crayfish, shrimps

involucral bract: one of several bracts that form a whorl below a flower or flower cluster

irruptive species: a species that occasionally appears in large numbers outside its usual range

K

key: a winged fruit, usually of an ash or maple; also called a "samara"

L

larva: immature forms of an animal that differ from the adult

leaflet: a division of a compound leaf

lenticel: a slightly raised portion of bark where the cells are packed more loosely, allowing for gas exchange with the atmosphere

lobate: having each toe individually webbed

lobe: a projecting part of a leaf or flower, usually rounded

M

metabolic rate: the rate of chemical processes in an organism

metamorphosis: the developmental transformation of an animal from larval to sexually mature adult stage

midden: the pile of cone scales found on the territories of tree squirrels, usually under a favourite tree

molt: when an animal sheds old feathers, fur or skin, in order to replace them with new growth

montane: of mountainous regions

myccorhizal fungi: fungi that has a mutually beneficial relationship with the roots of some seed plants

N

neotropical migrant: a bird that nests in North America, but overwinters in the New World tropics

nocturnal: active primarily at night

node: a slightly enlarged section of a stem where leaves or branches originate

nudibranch: sea slug

nutlet: a small, hard, single-seeded fruit that remains closed

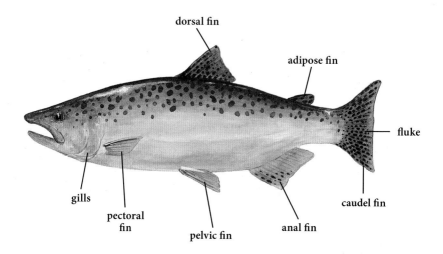

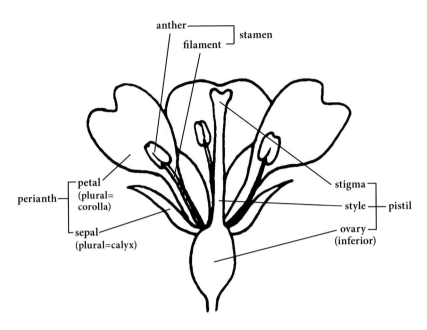

0

omnivorous: feeding on both plants and animals

ovoid: egg-shaped

P

palmate: leaflets, lobes or veins arranged around a single point, like the fingers on a hand (e.g., maple leaf)

pappus: the modified calyx of composite flowers (e.g., asters or daisies), consisting of awns, scales or bristles at the apex of the achene

parasite: a relationship between 2 species in which one benefits at the expense of the other

patagium: skin forming a flight membrane

pelage: the fur or hair of mammals

perennial: a plant that lives for several years

petal: a member of the inside ring of modified flower leaves, usually brightly coloured or white

phenology: stages of growth as influenced by climate

photosynthesis: conversion of CO_2 and water into sugars via energy of the sun

phyllary: a type of specialized bract found below the flower head in plants of the aster family (Asteraceae)

pinniped: a marine mammal with limbs that are modified to form flippers; a seal, sea-lion or walrus

pioneer species: a plant species that is capable of colonizing an otherwise unvegetated area; one of the first species to take hold in a disturbed area

piscivorous: fish-eating

pishing: a noise made to attract birds

pistil: the female organ of a flower, usually consisting of an ovary, style and stigma

plastic species: a species that can adapt to a wide range of conditions

plastron: the lower part of a turtle or tortoise shell, which covers the abdomen

poikilothermic: having a body temperature that is the same as the external environment and varies with it

pollen: the tiny grains produced in a plant's anthers and which contain the male reproductive cells

pollen cone: male cone that produces pollen

polyandry: a mating strategy in which one female mates with several males

pome: a fruit with a core, e.g., apple

precocial: animals who are active and independent at birth or hatching

prehensile: able to grasp

proboscis: the elongated tubular and flexible mouthpart of many insects

R

ray flower: in a composite flower (e.g., aster, daisy or sunflower), a type of flower usually with long, colourful petals that collectively make up the outer ring of petals (the centre of a composite flower is composed of disk flowers)

redd: spawing nest for fish

resinous: bearing resin, usually causing stickiness

rhinopores: tentacle-like sensory structures on the head of a nudibranch (sea slug)

rhizome: a horizontal underground stem

rictal bristles: hair-like feathers found on the faces of some birds

riparian: on the bank of a river or other watercourse

rookery: a colony of nests

runner: a slender stolon or prostrate stem that roots at the nodes or the tip

S

samara: a dry, winged fruit with usually only a single seed (e.g., maple or ash); also called a "key"

salmonid: a member of the Salmonidae family of fishes; includes trout, char, salmon, whitefish and grayling

schizocarp: a type of fruit that splits at maturity into 2 or more parts, each with a single seed

scutes: individual plates on a turtle's shell

seed cone: female cone that produces seeds

sepal: the outer, usually green, leaf-like structures that protect the flower bud and are located at the base of an open flower

silicle: a fruit of the mustard family (Brassicaceae) that is 2-celled and usually short, wide and often flat

silique: a long, thin fruit with many seeds; characteristic of some members of the mustard family (Brassicaceae)

sorus (pl. sori): a collection of sporangia under a fern frond; in some lichens and fungi, a structure that produces pores

spadix: a fleshy spike with many small flowers

spathe: a leaf-like sheath that surrounds a spadix

spur: a pointed projection

stamen: the pollen-bearing organ of a flower

stigma: a receptive tip in a flower that receives pollen

stolon: a long branch or stem that runs along the ground and often propagates more plants

subnivean: below the surface of the snow

substrate: the surface on which an organism grows; the material that makes up a streambed (e.g., sand or gravel)

suckering: a method of tree and shrub reproduction in which shoots arise from an underground stem

syrinx: a bird's vocal organ

T

taproot: the main, large root of a plant from which smaller roots arise, e.g., carrot

tendril: a slender, clasping or twining outgrowth from a stem or a leaf

tepal: a sepal or petal; used when both structures look very much alike and are not easily distinguished

terrestrial: land frequenting

torpor: a state of physical inactivity

tragus: a prominent structure of the outer ear of a bat

tubercule: a round nodule or warty outgrowth

tubular flower: a type of flower in which all or some of the petals are fused together at the base

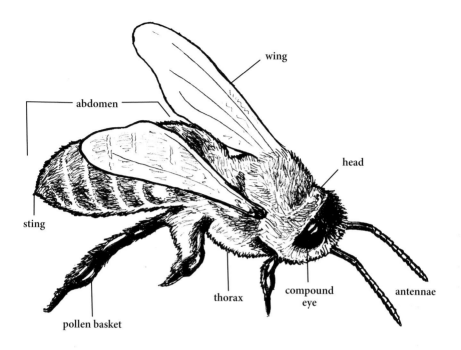

tundra: a high-altitude ecological zone at the northernmost limits of plant growth, where plants are reduced to shrubby or mat-like growth

tympanum: eardrum; the hearing organ of a frog

U

ungulate: an animal that has hooves

V

ventral: of or on the abdomen (belly)

vermiculations: wavy-patterned makings

vertebrate: an animal possessing a backbone

vibrissae: bristle-like feathers growing around the beak of birds to aid in catching insects

W

whorl: a circle of leaves or flowers around a stem

woolly: bearing long or matted hairs

REFERENCES

Acorn, John, and Ian Sheldon. 2001. *Bugs of British Columbia*. Lone Pine Publishing, Edmonton, AB.

Acorn, John, and Ian Sheldon. 2006. *Butterflies of British Columbia*. Lone Pine Publishing, Edmonton, AB.

B.C. Ministry of the Environment. *B.C. Fish Facts Factsheets*. http://www.env.gov.bc.ca/wld/fishhabitats/fishfactsheets.html

Bezener, Andy, and Linda Kershaw. 1999. *Rocky Mountain Nature Guide*. Lone Pine Publishing, Edmonton, AB.

Campbell, Wayne, and Gregory Kennedy. 2009. *Birds of British Columbia*. Lone Pine Publishing, Edmonton, AB.

Eder, Tamara, and Don Pattie. 2001. *Mammals of British Columbia*. Lone Pine Publishing, Edmonton, AB.

Farrar, John Liard. 1995. *Trees in Canada*. Fitzhenry and Whiteside Limited and the Canadian Forest Service, Ottawa, ON.

Leatherwood, Stephen, and Randall R. Reeves. 1983. *The Sierra Club Handbook of Whales and Dolphins*. Sierra Club Books, San Francisco, CA.

MacKinnon, A., L. Kershaw, J. Arnason, P. Owen, A. Karst and F. Hamersley-Chambers. 2009. *Edible and Medicinal Plants of Canada*. Lone Pine Publishing, Edmonton, AB.

National Audubon Society. 1998. *Field Guide to North American Fishes, Whales & Dophins*. Chanticleer Press, Toronto, ON.

Parish, Roberta, Ray Coupé and Dennis Lloyd. 1996. *Plants of Southern Interior British Columbia and the Inland Northwest*. B.C. Ministry of Forests and Lone Pine Publishing, Edmonton, AB.

Pojar, Jim, and Andy MacKinnon. 1994. *Plants of Coastal British Columbia Including Washington, Oregon and Alaska*. B.C. Ministry of Forests and Lone Pine Publishing, Edmonton, AB.

Sheldon, Ian. 1998. *Seashore of British Columbia*. Lone Pine Publishing, Edmonton, AB.

Sibley, David Allen. 2000 *The Sibley Field Guide to Birds of North America*. Alfred A. Knopf, NY.

Spalding, David A.E. 1998. *Whales of the West Coast*. Harbour Publishing, Madeira Park, BC.

St. John, Alan. 2002. *Reptiles of the Northwest: California to Alaska, Rockies to the Coast*. Lone Pine Publishing, Edmonton, AB.

Sullivan, M., D. Propst and W. Gould. 2009. *Fish of the Rockies*. Lone Pine Publishing, Edmonton, AB.

INDEX

Names in **boldface** type indicate primary species.

ABOUT THE AUTHOR

Erin McCloskey spent her formative years observing nature from atop her horse while growing up in the countryside of rural Canada. Erin received her BSc with distinction in environmental and conservation sciences, majoring in conservation biology and management from the University of Alberta. An active campaigner for the protection of endangered species and spaces, Erin has collaborated with various NGOs and has been involved in numerous endangered species conservation projects around the world. Erin began working as an editor with Lone Pine Publishing in 1996. Since 2000 she has freelanced as a writer and editor for several magazine and book publishers focused on nature, travel, scientific research and even alternative healthcare. Erin is the author of *The Bradt Travel Guide to Argentina, Ireland Flying High, Canada Flying High, Hawaii from the Air* and co-author/editor for the *Green Volunteers* guidebook series. Erin is also the author of the *Washington and Oregon Nature Guide, Southern California Nature Guide,* and *Northern California Nature Guide* and *Bear Attacks* for Lone Pine Publishing.